The Long Recon

MW00781247

A century and a half after the Civil War, Americans are still dealing with the legacies of the conflict and Reconstruction, including the many myths and legends spawned by these events. *The Long Reconstruction: The Post-Civil War South in History, Film, and Memory* brings together history and popular culture to explore how the events of this era have been remembered.

Looking at popular cinema across the last hundred years, *The Long Reconstruction* uncovers central themes in the history of Reconstruction, including violence and terrorism; the experiences of African Americans and those of women and children; the Lost Cause ideology; and the economic reconstruction of the American South.

Analyzing influential films such as *The Birth of a Nation* and *Gone with the Wind*, as well as more recent efforts such as *Cold Mountain* and *Lincoln,* the authors show how the myths surrounding Reconstruction have impacted American culture.

This engaging book is essential reading for anyone interested in the history of Reconstruction, historical memory, and popular culture.

Frank J. Wetta is Lecturer, Department of History and Senior Fellow, Center for History Politics and Policy, Kean University. He is the author of *The Louisiana Scalawags: Politics, Race, and Terrorism during the Civil War and Reconstruction* (2012).

Martin A. Novelli is Professor of Film, History, and Humanities at Ocean County College, New Jersey. He also teaches film history at the University of the Arts, Philadelphia.

The Long Reconstruction

The Post-Civil War South in History, Film, and Memory

Frank J. Wetta and
Martin A. Novelli

Routledge
Taylor & Francis Group

NEW YORK AND LONDON

First published 2014
by Routledge, 711 Third Avenue, New York, NY 10017

Simultaneously published in the UK
by Routledge, 2 Park Square, Milton Park, Abingdon, Oxon OX14 4RN

Routledge is an imprint of the Taylor & Francis Group, an
informa business

Library of Congress Cataloging-in-Publication Data

Wetta, Frank Joseph, 1942–
   The long reconstruction : the post-Civil War south in
history, film, and memory / Frank Wetta and Martin Novelli.
      pages cm
   1. Reconstruction (U.S. history, 1865–1877)—Social
aspects.   2. Popular culture—Southern States—History—
19th century.   3. United States—History—Civil War,
1861–1865—Motion pictures and the war.   4. Collective
memory—Southern States   5. Southern States—Social life and
customs—1865–   6. Memory—Social aspects—Southern
States.   7. United States—History—Civil War, 1861–
1865—Influence.   8. United States—History—Civil War,
1861–1865—Social aspects.   I. Novelli, Martin.   II. Title.
   E668.W48 2013
   973.8—dc23
   2013010029

ISBN: 978-0-415-89464-7 (hbk)
ISBN: 978-0-415-89465-4 (pbk)
ISBN: 978-0-203-12226-6 (ebk)

Typeset in Sabon by Apex CoVantage, LLC

Printed and Bound in the United States of America by
Edwards Brothers Malloy

For Rachel and Mary

—Frank J. Wetta

For my wife Lisa, for my sons Max and Jake, and for my brother Lawrence

—Martin A. Novelli

Contents

Chronology

The Civil War and Reconstruction are commonly thought of as occurring in sequence—first came the war and then Reconstruction. Actually, the war and the struggle over Reconstruction took place simultaneously until 1865. After the Confederate surrender in 1865, the contest over the future of the South continued for at least another twelve years. Some would argue the struggle continued much longer—perhaps another hundred years. The chronology below divides this history into distinct phases that marked significant events in the process of Reconstruction. (See Chapter 1 "The Night They Drove Old Dixie Down": Constructing Reconstruction History.)

I ABRAHAM LINCOLN'S WARTIME RECONSTRUCTION: 1861–1865

The process of Reconstruction during Lincoln's presidency was fluid, reflecting the president's belief that his primary duty was to save the Union. He based his Reconstruction policies on his expansive concept of the war powers of the presidency.

1861   *August*: The First Confiscation Act authorized Federal seizure of any slaves used in support of the rebellion.

1862   *February*: Republican Senator Charles Sumner of Massachusetts outlined his state suicide theory.

April: With the Southern Democrats gone, a Republican-dominated Congress freed the slaves living in the District of Columbia.

June: Congress banned slavery in the territories. Lincoln appointed military governors in Louisiana, Tennessee, and North Carolina.

September: Lincoln issued the Preliminary Emancipation Proclamation, hoping that Southern Unionists would take advantage of the opportunity to effect a return to the Union.

1863   *January*: Lincoln issued the Emancipation Proclamation.

April: The Appalachian region of western Virginia "seceded" from the rebel state Virginia and joined the Union as a free state. The new state constitution provided for the gradual emancipation of slaves.

December: Lincoln, hoping to entice rebels back into the Union, issued the Amnesty and Reconstruction proclamation. He also moved to establish Unionist-based state governments in occupied areas of Louisiana, Arkansas, Virginia, and North Carolina.

1864   *July*: Congress passed the Wade–Davis Bill as a protest against Lincoln's plan of Reconstruction. They argued that he was moving too fast. Lincoln responded with a "pocket veto."

August: Congress reacted to Lincoln's veto with the Wade–Davis Manifesto attacking his Reconstruction policies.

November: Lincoln won a second term in office along with Andrew Johnson, a Southern Unionist and pro-war Democrat, as his new vice president. Sherman began his march through Georgia. (*Gone with the Wind* and *Cold Mountain,* both novels adapted as motion pictures, provide vivid images of the Southern home front during this period as experienced by white women. See Chapter 3 "Let's Make a Start": Women and Reconstruction.)

1865 *March*: Freedmen's Bureau was established to assist with the transition of the ex-slaves from bondage to freedom. Lincoln's Second Inaugural Address seemed to indicate to many both at the time and afterwards that he favored a quick restoration of the Southern states with limited political reform and humane treatment of the rebels: "With malice toward none, with charity for all, with firmness in the right as God gives us to see the right, let us strive on to finish the work we are in, to bind up the nation's wounds, to care for him who shall have borne the battle and for his widow and his orphan, to do all which may achieve and cherish a just and lasting peace among ourselves and with all nations." Andrew Johnson appeared drunk at the inauguration ceremonies.

II   ANDREW JOHNSON AND PRESIDENTIAL RECONSTRUCTION: 1865–1868

Johnson became president upon Lincoln's assassination. The new president was strongly opposed to secession, but, unlike Lincoln, he proved no friend of the freedmen. "Damn the Negroes, I am fighting those traitorous aristocrats, their masters," he exclaimed. Southerners were at first unsure of what impact Lincoln's death would have on the defeated South. For their part, the Republicans initially saw Johnson as an ally. (See Chapter 2, Lincoln "Unmurdered": Reconstruction Alternatives and Counterfactuals.)

1865 *April*: Robert E. Lee surrendered the Army of Northern Virginia. In General Order #9, Lee bid farewell to the men of the Army of Northern Virginia. The address contained essential elements of what would become the Lost Cause ideology—references to Southern fortitude, duty and "County," and submission only to impossible odds.

May: Johnson laid out his own plan of Reconstruction—a process, he contended, that embodied Lincoln's goal of a quick restoration of the Union.

November: Mississippi passed a "black code" designed to control the activities, labor, and mobility of ex-slaves, in effect restoring aspects of the old slave codes.

December: Johnson announced that the former rebel states were now reconstructed and restored to the Union. But Congress refused to recognize the Johnson state governments. Congress established a Joint Committee on Reconstruction to inquire into conditions in the South. The Thirteenth Amendment abolished slavery. (For a discussion of black self-emancipation and the issue of race and memory see Chapter 4 "Sunshine Headin' My Way": Memories of Reconstruction in Black and White.)

1866   *February*: Johnson vetoed Freedmen's Bureau Bill.

April: Congress enacted first Civil Rights Act over Johnson's veto. Virginia journalist Edward A. Pollard published *The Lost Cause: A New Southern History of the War of the Confederates.*

May: Ex-rebel soldiers in Tennessee established the Ku Klux Klan. Memphis was the scene of a widely reported race riot. The anti-Republican, anti-Reconstruction insurgency soon spread across the South in a variety of informal or paramilitary organizations. (See Chapter 6 "I Am Vengeful and I Shall Not Sleep": The Civil War and the Legacy of Violence during Reconstruction.)

June: Supreme Court weakened black civil rights in Slaughter-House Cases ruling.

July: Ex-rebels in New Orleans rioted against Southern Unionists (scalawags) and their black allies.

August: Johnson began his "swing around the circle"—a series of speeches attacking the Republicans over Reconstruction policy.

November: Republicans won significant victories in the Congressional elections.

III   CONGRESSIONAL RECONSTRUCTION: 1868–1877

In the face of Johnson's continuing opposition, the Radical Republicans and their allies moved to initiate a Congressional program of Reconstruction in March 1867 and in July 1868 that would ensure passage of the Fourteenth Amendment, black civil rights and loyal (read Republican) governments in the states of the former Confederacy. Central to the Congressional plan was the rejection of the Johnson-approved state government and the division of the former Confederacy (excepting Tennessee) into five military districts.

1867   *March–July*: The Republicans passed three Reconstruction acts despite Johnson's vetoes. Importantly, Congress required the ex-Confederate states to ratify the Fourteenth Amendment. The Republicans were now free to move ahead without Johnson obstructionism. The war over Reconstruction, however, was far from over.

1868   *February*: The Republicans, fed up with Johnson's continued attempts to thwart Radical Reconstruction, brought impeachment charges designed to remove him from office. "Instead of cooperating with Congress, by execution of laws passed by it, he has thwarted and delayed their execution, and sought to bring the laws and the legislative power into contempt," Republican Senator John Sherman of Ohio charged.
May: Although the Senate voted for acquittal, Johnson was now politically impotent. Congress continued with its plan of Reconstruction.
June: Reformed states Arkansas, North Carolina, South Carolina, Georgia, Florida, Alabama, and Louisiana were readmitted to the Union under the congressional requirements.
July: Fourteenth Amendment was ratified.

1869   *August*: Tennessee elected an all-white Democratic state government.

1870   *February*: Hiram Revels of Mississippi became the first African American elected to the U. S. Senate.

    March: Virginia, Mississippi, Texas, and Georgia were readmitted to the Union in accord with Congressional requirements. The Fifteenth Amendment, designed to protect black voting, was adopted: "The right of citizens of the United States to vote shall be not be denied or abridged by the United States or by any State on account of race, color, or previous condition of servitude." Southern state governments under Democrat control, however, schemed to find ways to undermine the law— poll taxes, literacy tests, and other means to restrict or eliminate black suffrage.

    May. Congress, concerned about the insurgency in the South, passed the Enforcement Act—a law aimed at suppressing the Ku Klux Klan and other anti-Reconstruction insurgents.

1871   *November*: Five African Americans were elected to the U.S. House of Representatives: Benjamin S. Turner (Alabama); Josiah T. Walls (Florida); Robert Brown Elliot, Joseph H. Rainey, and Robert Carlos DeLarge (South Carolina).

1872   *May*: Through the Amnesty Act, Congress restored the civil rights of ex-rebels (with the exception of their military and political leaders). Congress also terminated the Freedmen's Bureau.

1873   *April*: The Supreme Court's conservative ruling in the Slaughter-House cases weakened the new Fourteenth Amendment relative to black rights.

1874   *November*: The Democrats staged a comeback in the Congressional elections and took control of Congress. The handwriting was now on the wall for the eventual termination of Reconstruction.

1875   *March*: Congress passed the Civil Rights Act of 1875—a law designed to protect equal rights for blacks in public accommodations and jury service. It was one of the final efforts to effect genuine reform in the South.
October–November: The conservative Redeemers seized power in Mississippi through violence and intimidation.

1876   *November*: The presidential election of 1876 pit the Republican, Rutherford B. Hayes, against a Democrat, Samuel J. Tilden. Gross irregularities in the popular vote count in Oregon, South Carolina, Louisiana, and Florida forced the election into the House of Representatives.

IV   THE UNDOING OF RECONSTRUCTION: 1877 AND BEYOND

In time, the determination of the North to persist with Reconstruction softened. The Northern retreat reflected the pressures of continued resistance in the South, Democratic opposition at the polls, and, ultimately, the North's shallow commitment to the protection of black civil rights.

1877   *February*: A meeting at the black-owned Wormley's Hotel in Washington, DC settled the disputed election of 1876. In "The Compromise of 1877," the Republicans got the presidency and the "Redeemers" got the South. Although about 30,000 Federal troops remained in Florida, Louisiana, and South Carolina, the compromisers understood that the soldiers would remain but not intervene to support the so-called carpetbag state governments in the push and shove of Southern politics. The Republicans abandoned support of the last "carpetbag" holdouts in Louisiana and Florida. The South was "redeemed." Reconstruction in what may be considered its formal phase was over. And Congress removed the last legal restrictions on ex-rebels. The "informal secession" was over.

1883   The Supreme Court ruled that the equal-accommoda-
       tions sections of the Civil Rights Acts of 1875 were
       unconstitutional. Speaking of the Redeemer victory
       in the battle for Reconstruction, Lucius Q.C. Lamar
       (who had authored the Mississippi Ordinance of Seces-
       sion and who later served on the U.S. Supreme Court,
       1888–1893) wrote that the white South had defeated
       its Reconstruction enemies: "We have no enemy in our
       front."

1890– *Disfranchisement*: The governments of the South, con-
1908   trolled by the Redeemer Democrats, moved to elimi-
       nate the Republican black vote through the poll tax,
       the grandfather clauses, felon disfranchisement, literacy
       tests, and other means. In Louisiana the number of black
       voters fell from 130,334 to 1,342. African Americans in
       the South would not return to the polls in significant
       numbers until after the passage of the Voting Rights Act
       of 1965.

1896   *Segregation* (the "Jim Crow" system): In *Plessey v. Fer-
       guson* (1896), the U.S. Supreme ruled that "separate but
       equal" racial segregation in public accommodations was
       legal under the Fourteenth Amendment. State by state,
       "Redemption" reversed the brief period of integration
       enacted by the Reconstruction state governments. Even-
       tually, formal segregation touched a wide range of situ-
       ations: schools, trains, buses, movie theaters, swimming
       pools, water fountains, grave yards, and more.

1913– *Reconciliation*: Confederate and Union veterans, now in
1963   their seventies and eighties, returned to the Gettysburg
       battlefield in July 1913. "The Grand Reunion" occurred
       in a spirit of comradeship and shared experience for the
       fiftieth anniversary of the engagement. There, President
       Woodrow Wilson spoke of North–South reconciliation:
       "We have found one another again as brothers and

comrades in arms, enemies no longer, generous friends rather, our battles long past, the quarrel forgotten—except that we shall not forget the splendid valor."

The centennial anniversary of the battle in 1963 reaffirmed the image of the Civil War as a brothers' war over the nature of the Union. The ceremony ignored slavery as the essential cause of the Civil War. Further, Reconstruction became the "tragic era" in popular memory in the North as well as the South. Southerners had won the memory war (see Chapter 7 "A Gallant Soldier and a Christian Gentleman": The Reconciliation of North and South" and Chapter 8 "Princess of the Moon: The Lost Cause, Reconstruction, and Southern Memory.")

1 "The Night They Drove Old Dixie Down"

Constructing Reconstruction History

And the high school band played "Dixieland"
While they tore our tattered flags and banners down.

Warren Zevon, 1991

When a reader asked on *Historum* (a website devoted to history book reviews and discussions) how many books had been published on the American Civil War, this was the answer: "I think I read there are like 60,000 (+)." "That's a lot of books," was the questioner's reply.[1] Indeed, that *is* a lot of books. But publications about the war actually total a great deal more. Civil War scholar James McPherson estimated in 1996 that "the number approaches six figures and continues to grow at an astounding rate."[2] On the other hand, Reconstruction per se has attracted far less attention. A research guide to works on Reconstruction history published in 2000 included fewer than 3,000 entries.[3] The number of books is not small, yet, unlike the war stories, Reconstruction, especially important as it relates to race in America, has not held the high ground of historical memory. If Reconstruction lacks the vast audience and Homeric qualities of the Civil War, nevertheless, it has been a "dark and bloody ground" on which Northerners and Southerners, both white and black, including historians, novelists, and filmmakers (even songwriters), have battled over the its history, meaning, and memory.

Reconstruction as a coherent period lasted from 1861 to 1877, longer than the Civil War itself. It can be argued, however, that Reconstruction lasted well beyond the traditional ending date. Did it actually conclude in 1890 with the onset of the Age of Segregation and Disfranchisement? (African-American historian W. E. B. Du Bois, for example, opened his history of Reconstruction in 1860 and concluded it in 1880.) Perhaps the end of Reconstruction came with the conclusion of the civil rights movement in the 1970s.[4] In fact, the termination of Reconstruction was an ever-receding horizon.

There are three essential themes in the history of Reconstruction: 1) *reform*—the North's attempt to reorder the political and social system of the rebel states; 2) *reaction*—the South's response to the political, economic, and social consequences of the war; and 3) *memory*—the contest over the memory and meaning of the events.

HISTORY IN THE INTERROGATIVE MOOD

In developing a screenplay, a writer will often produce a "backstory"—a literary device that assumes that the characters in the film have biographies. The idea is to give the actors some sense of context and the motivation of the characters in the movie. In this sense, historians also write backstories based on the recovery and evaluation of evidence and memory. In trying to understand Reconstruction as event, as experience, and as myth, it is helpful to understand, in brief, what Reconstruction meant and the issues it presented to the people who lived through it.

In January 1861 in *DeBow's Review*, a pro-Southern magazine published in New Orleans, Louisiana, the editor stated that: "Any remedy [for the secession crisis] ... looking ... to a reconstruction, must be based upon the idea of the equality of sections as well as of States."[5] He was referring to a reconstruction (that is, a reunion) based on a Southern definition of "equality." Throughout the war, Southerners used the term "reconstructionists" to refer to those inclined toward reconciliation (on Southern terms) with the North. By the end of 1861, however, reconstruction came to mean something well beyond what J.D.B. DeBow or other Southerners had in mind. It would become a complex, frustrating, evolving racial and political struggle and the developing Federal policy toward the Confederate South.

Reconstruction lasted through the Civil War and then, after the surrender of the Confederate armies in 1865, for at least another twelve years. Even though Reconstruction commonly refers to the period in American history from 1865 to 1877, it more broadly encompassed a set of events and problems associated with the attempt both during and after the Civil War to reunite the nation and reform the South. It is a story intertwined with the war. The attempt to reorder the race relations of Southern society occasioned by the progress of the war and formal emancipation resulted in a long-term fight over the meaning of black equality.

Beyond the immediate issues of secession and emancipation, the racial and political struggle that defined the sixteen years of the American Civil War and Reconstruction era remained in vital ways unresolved, continuing to vex the nation for generations.

Reconstruction occurred over 135 years ago yet its legacy and its arguments persist to our own day. The leading historian of Reconstruction today, Columbia University professor Eric Foner, stated that the unfinished business of Reconstruction would not remain relevant "so long as the issues central to Reconstruction remain unresolved—the balance of power in the federal system, the place of black Americans in national life, and the relationship between economic and political democracy."[6] So, we are not yet finished with Reconstruction.

STILL HAVING THE SAME FIGHTS

On July 21, 1979, "The China Grove Committee to Smash the Klan," an *ad hoc* group related to the Workers Viewpoint Organization (WVO, a group of young black and white radicals) confronted the Klan in China Grove, a hamlet sixty miles southeast of Greensboro, North Carolina. The Klan had planned to show *The Birth of a Nation* at the local community center as a recruitment tool; however, the radicals disrupted the Klan meeting, forcing the Klansmen, although armed with M16s and other weapons, to retreat into the building where they intended to show the movie. The radicals then burned a rebel flag in defiance and taunted the Klansmen, calling them "a slimly pack of cowards."

The China Grove incident set the stage for a violent confrontation four months later in Greensboro. In the early afternoon of November 3, 1979, the Ku Klux Klan, including some of their friends in the American Nazi Party, confronted the WVO—later renamed the Communist Workers Party (CWP). The radicals were preparing for a "Death to the Klan March" near a public housing project. After a brief skirmish with the organizers, the Klansmen and the Nazis fired into the demonstrators leaving five dead and several wounded. One or more of the marchers fired back but without effect. All this was recorded on a local news channel videotape.

Nearly thirty years later, in 2005, the Greensboro Truth and Reconciliation Commission held a series of community hearings to explore the origins and consequences of the shootings and to encourage community "healing." Those who testified before the commission included participants in the Greensboro affair, community activists, judges, prosecutors, ministers, police officers, and historians. At the hearings, two men testified relative to the China Grove incident that foreshadowed the "massacre" in Greensboro.

Paul Bermanzohn, M.D., a New Yorker and the son of Holocaust survivors, and former member of the CWP, was partially paralyzed on his left side after taking a bullet in his forehead on the day of the Greensboro march. He stated that he and some of his comrades had disrupted the Klan's movie night and then burned a Confederate flag:

> When I called the Klan a bunch of cowards, there is nothing wrong with that—that's right. Call them murder[er]s the truth is on the video tape.

The City Council (of China Grove) at that point, all white, had approved the use of the white Community Center for showing *The Birth of a Nation*, which is an old film which has been a recruitment film for the Klan from the beginning. Its first use was as a recruitment film. It was self-consciously made for that purpose.

What happened is that after we had marched twice around the building some people took the Confederate Flag that was standing in front ... And people burned it and that was a powerful statement, a powerful statement. Burning this Confederate Flag in front of this Klan rally said a lot.

Joseph Gorrell Pierce, a native Alabamian, farmer, and business owner, was the Grand Dragon of the Federated Knights of the Ku Klux Klan in 1979:

I've always had a direct link with the past by virtue of the fact that the doctor that was present on the day that my mother was born was General Jed Stewart's [*sic*] physician during the War Between the States.

So I have a direct tie with the past. And on those porches, the talk by the elderly people ... Sunday evenings they'd dip snuff and they talked about the Civil War and Reconstruction and how things used to be.

The older people spoke about Reconstruction and how the Klan overthrew the Reconstruction government. Of course we all know it was a horrible bad time for everybody, black or white, poor or rich, but there wasn't anybody rich except for the carpetbaggers. So as I got older and loved history, it was easy for me to study North Carolina history, it was easy for me to study Southern history. And down this road I went.

We had purchased the movie *The Birth of a Nation* and I had read the book by Thomas Dixon, *The Klansman* [*sic*] which the movie is based on. And the book was interesting. And I'd never saw the film but I'd heard of it.

So we purchased the movie, the original uncut version. We even had the soundtrack where they played the piano in the theatre. And it was a tinted version, so the battle scenes were tinted in red. And the movie is both amusing to me and it is a historical movie. I would urge anybody to see that movie.

Now, our purpose was to show the movie was in the historical sense. And of course, the movie glorified the Klan, so naturally we wanted a little good publicity.[7]

The Greensboro shootings were the result of a volatile mix of racism, activism, and historical memory. Bermanzohn mistakenly believed that D.W. Griffith had purposely made the film in 1915 to recruit members for the Klan; Pierce mistakenly believed that the film was an accurate representation of Reconstruction. In essence, this was an argument over history and its meaning. The Truth and Reconciliation Commission report referred to the history of this event as "a richly complex story." They reasoned that "the truth" was "necessarily imperfect" but believed that in time a "collective truth" would emerge.

Despite attempts to reconcile conflicting memories, the contest has continued. On March 12, 2012, vandals stole a bronze bust of Confederate General Nathan Bedford Forrest (1821–1877) from a city park in Selma, Alabama. Forrest, a slave owner, slave trader, military superstar, and rebel hero, is one of the most controversial figures in the history of the American Civil War and Reconstruction. He has been accused, on good evidence, of the massacre of black prisoners of war following the Battle of Fort Pillow in 1864. On top of that, he was the first "grand wizard" of the Reconstruction-era Ku Klux Klan. When the Friends of Forrest, Inc., a society dedicated to his memory, attempted to erect a new monument, protestors stopped the construction, and a legal and media battle ensured. Malika Sanders-Fortier, who was involved with the Slavery and Civil War Museum in Selma, set up an online petition against the Forrest monument. "Here we are on the 150th anniversary of the Civil War," she wrote, "and we're still having the same fights."[8]

CONTESTING THE PAST

Whose history is it anyway? Who gets to tell the story? Why is the past contested? Why are there competing schools of interpretation? What historian Tony Judt asks regarding the uses of the past and the Holocaust applies to the history of Reconstruction as well: "Who has the right to design an exhibition, assign meaning to a battlefield, inscribe a plinth or a plaque? These are the tactical skirmishes in the greater cultural conflict over identity: national, regional, linguistic, religious, racial, ethnic, sexual."[9] Who, then, gets to assign meaning to Reconstruction? What is true about Reconstruction history, and what are the uses of Reconstruction history? History is a dialogue about the past, a conversation among historians, in particular, and the public in general. Revisionist historians ask new questions, approach the past from new perspectives, reexamine or discover new evidence, and create alternate narratives. This is the essence of historical writing—point and counterpoint. This is not to say that the truth is unknowable, but as the Greensboro Truth and Reconciliation Commission put it, the "truth" about the past is "necessarily complex."

THE ORTHODOX SCHOOL

Columbia University professor William Archibald Dunning (1859–1926) was the founding father of the orthodox or traditional historical interpretation of Reconstruction and a major influence in the history profession, serving as the president of the American Historical Association in 1913 and the American Political Science Association in 1922. He was writing near-contemporary history and his view reflected the body of opinion about Reconstruction. Despite his dedication to the professionalism of historical inquiry, a patina of racial prejudice and political bias overlaid his professionalism. For Dunning's generation, the Civil War and Reconstruction was a part of "family history"—living memory.[10] His *Reconstruction: Political and*

Economic appeared in 1907 only thirty years after the Compromise of 1877. Dunning tailored the orthodox theme that would dominate the interpretation of the period for the next fifty years. "To the people of the North ... [victory] meant that their passionate demand of 1861 had been realized—the union was preserved"; he wrote, "to the people of the South it meant that their bitterest forebodings of that year had come true—they were subjected to an alien power."[11] The result of the triumph of the Radical Republicans and the imposition of their policies was the creation of a Southern dystopia.

Dunning designed the pattern for a series of academic and popular histories portraying Reconstruction as a "tragic era," reflecting a pro-Southern, anti-black, anti-Reconstruction bias.[12] Here is the interpretation in its essentials: White Southerners, fighting for states' rights, having accepted defeat on the battlefield, were subjected to rule by ignorant black field hands controlled on the state level by unscrupulous scalawags (poor white Southern race traitors) and carpetbaggers (money-grubbing Northern or outside whites). Vengeful Northern Radical Republicans puppet masters controlled the Southern state house gangs from Washington. Unable to tolerate the corrupt domination by their political enemies and social inferiors, and determined to restore decency to the South, white Southerners resorted in frustration to the Ku Klux Klan and other paramilitary organizations. "The deep dread of negro domination under the auspices of invincible national power," Dunning wrote, "impelled thousands of serious and respectable whites to look for some means of mitigation ... in the methods of the secret societies."[13] This view of Reconstruction informed the dominant narrative about the subject from the turn of the century until at least the mid-1950s.

THE REVISIONIST SCHOOL

Revisionist historians pull at the loose threads of established interpretations. In this case, Du Bois began tugging on the "truth" of Reconstruction in an essay entitled "Reconstruction and its

Benefits" in the *American Historical Review* in 1910.[14] Again, in 1935, he attacked the orthodox view in a lengthy book entitled *Black Reconstruction: An Essay Toward a History of the Part Which Black Folk Played in the Attempt to Reconstruct Democracy in America, 1860–1880.* He charged that Dunning and his followers had distorted, even lied, about the history of Reconstruction. They had assumed that black people were ignorant, lazy, dishonest, and "responsible for bad government during Reconstruction." Because of this, they had ignored the real achievements and revolutionary potential of the postwar Civil War years:

> White historians have ascribed the faults and failures of Reconstruction to Negro ignorance and corruption. But the Negro insists that it was Negro loyalty and the Negro vote alone that restored the South to the Union; established the new democracy, both for white and black ..."[15]

Du Bois's position did not gain general currency. The argument was culturally and politically premature and its Marxist proclivities were suspect but it did prepare the battleground for a powerful revisionist offensive against the Dunningites.

Influenced by personal values and experience, changing views of race following World War II, and the civil rights movement, revisionist historians (among them John Hope Franklin, whose personal experiences with prejudice help shape his view of Reconstruction, and Kenneth Stampp) constructed a counter-narrative to the orthodox interpretation. They, like Du Bois, were critical of what the Dunningites had done (vilify southern Republicans and justify the Klan) and what they had failed to do (give black people and their allies credit for the benefits of Reconstruction).

They picked up where Du Bois left off. Book by book, article by article, this new generation of historians dismantled orthodox Reconstruction. They emphasized its opportunities and described its victories. In 1969, historian David Levering Lewis stated, "the war against racist Reconstruction historiography had been won."[16]

In 1987, Eric Foner, in his magisterial, seven-hundred page survey of the history of the 1860s and 1870s, argued that Reconstruction was a powerful and deeply important story of an "unfinished revolution" in American life. If Reconstruction in its own time failed to fully transform the South (and the nation), "the institutions created or consolidated after the Civil War— the black family, school, and church—provided the base from which the modern civil rights revolution sprang. And for its legal strategy, the movement turned to the laws and amendments of Reconstruction."[17] Revisionist scholars can proclaim a decisive victory in the battle of the books (the Dunning interpretation is now thoroughly discredited in academia). They have had less success in the battle for the popular mind.

THE PERSISTENCE OF MYTH

The memory of Reconstruction remains (especially in the white South) fixed on a set of historical and racial beliefs. This is due primarily to the effective dramatization presented in popular histories, novels, and films that deal with the Civil War and Reconstruction. The story as told by the Dunningite popularizers had all the elements of good melodrama—excitement, sentimentality, histrionics, pathos, and easily defined characters. It was told on a grand scale.

The Civil War may have higher entertainment value, but Reconstruction can hold its own when it comes to storytelling and its ability to incite motion. Hollywood, for its part, recognized the dramatic qualities inherent in Reconstruction. They understood that Reconstruction is, in its own right, a truly dramatic story. The whole second half of D. W. Griffith's silent film *The Birth of a Nation* (1915), Hollywood's first "blockbuster" movie is, for example, about Reconstruction.[18] The title card that introduces the Reconstruction segment reads: "This is an historical presentation of the Civil War and Reconstruction Period, and is not meant to reflect on any race or people of today." Of course, the movie did reflect on "race" and "people," and black leaders at the time, in particular, were outraged by the film's explicit racism. Among their issues was the film's outright justification for the Ku Klux Klan, an organization, one of the title cards reads, "that saved the South from the anarchy of black rule ..."

Calling on the same thematic approach and anti-Reconstruction bias as Griffith (his father was a Confederate colonel), Southern novelist Margaret Mitchell devoted the second half of *Gone with the Wind* (1936), a 1034-page, Pulitzer Prize-winning novel, to the economic hardships and supposed oppressions of the Reconstruction years. Her description of Antebellum planter society is only a prelude. The book is really about the ruination of the slaveholder's world through war and the hardships of Reconstruction. The burning of Atlanta (one of the most famous scenes in the film version of *Gone with the Wind*) comes one-third of the way into the book. Then, half way through the story, Mitchell writes, "The scourge of war had been followed by the *worst scourge* of Reconstruction" (emphasis added). "It was," she asserted, "a glorious spree for the gang which held Georgia by the throat. There was an orgy of grabbing and over all there was a cold cynicism about open theft in high places that was chilling to contemplate."[19]

Together, *The Birth of a Nation* and *Gone with the Wind* (including the film adaptation) have attracted an audience of millions. Warner publications, for instance, sold 650,000 copies of a special edition of *Gone with the Wind* between 1993 and 2007. Griffith and Mitchell, reflecting the conservative historical and racial assumptions of their time, presented fiction posing as history, yet both believed that their stories were essentially true to the historical experience. The vivid images of Reconstruction that they created represented a particular, yet enduring, understanding of Reconstruction. In important ways, both *The Birth of a Nation* and *Gone with the Wind* were the dramatic counterparts of the prevailing interpretation of Reconstruction in the historical profession. In time, that view would come under intense attack by revisionist historians, freed of the racial and class assumptions of the post-Civil War generation.

With such material to work with, the popularizers early on seized upon the era of Reconstruction. Indeed, the lasting effect of the Dunning interpretation owed less to the influence of early professional historians than to the work of popular writers, novelists, and Hollywood filmmakers. Thomas Dixon (1864–1946), D. W. Griffith (1875–1948), and Margaret Mitchell (1900–1949) dramatized and amplified the traditional story and its characters to such a degree that the work of academic revisionists has often gone unnoticed. Thomas Dixon (one-time actor; graduate student in history and politics at Johns Hopkins University; law student; North Carolina legislator; and Baptist minister) wrote three bestselling novels dealing with the history of Reconstruction and the Ku Klux Klan—*The Leopard's Spots: A Romance of the White Man's Burden* (1902), *The Clansman* (1905), and *The Traitor* (1907). His writing, as shown in *The Leopard's Spots,* "the greatest of all Dixon's propaganda works," according to one authority, had "all the logic of a lawyer, the social criticism of the reformer, the zeal of the religious prophet and the actor's sense of dramatic incident and timing."[20] Despite the verve and vigor of his prose, *The Leopard's Spots* is filled with cardboard characters, the denizens of the fictional town of Hambright, North Carolina. The principal figures include Sallie Worth ("a daughter of the old-fashioned South"), Charles Gaston (the brave and handsome former Confederate colonel), Nelse (a comic but faithful "darkie"), Tom Camp (the "nigger" hating poor white), and Allan McLeod (a scalawag). Despite the Victorian plots, the one-dimensional characters, and the crude racism, the original audience responded enthusiastically and his books are still in print and available on Amazon.com a hundred years later.

The Leopard's Spots and especially its companion volume, *The Clansman,* provided the scenario for *The Birth of a Nation.* The copyright title is, in fact, *The Birth of a Nation or the Clansman.* With the celluloid film tinted for dramatic effect and its symphonic score (the silent movie had live accompaniment) this stunning production presented the orthodox interpretation of Reconstruction with graphic brilliance. Writing in 1960 during the early stage of the civil rights movement, historian Everett Carter offered this judgment on *The Birth of a Nation* as history:

> It served the ugliest purposes of pseudo-art—giving people a reflection of their own prejudices, sentimental at best, vicious at worst, and a restatement of their easy explanations of the terrible complexities of their history as Americans. It demonstrated how easily and how successfully the art could pander to the sentimentality of the public; how effectively and profitably it could transfer melodrama from the stage and values from the novel.[21]

Here, film critic Roger Ebert, writing in 2003, assesses Griffith's work:

> [Yet] when it comes to his version of the Reconstruction era, he tells the story of the liberation of the slaves and its aftermath through the eyes of a Southerner who cannot view African-Americans as possible partners in American civilization. In the first half of the film the black characters are mostly ignored in the background. In the second half, Griffith dramatizes material in which white women are seen as the prey of lustful freed slaves, often urged on by evil white Northern carpetbaggers whose goal is to destroy and loot the South. The most exciting and technically accomplished sequence in the second half of the film is also the most disturbing, as a white family is under siege in a log cabin, attacked by blacks and their white exploiters, while the Ku Klux Klan rides to the rescue.[22]

The common wisdom regarding Reconstruction embedded in the works of Dunning and Dixon appeared again in Margaret Mitchell's historical novel. A mixture of romance and realism, the story centers on Scarlett O'Hara (a fascinating combination of one part liberated woman and one part Southern belle) and her life during and after the Civil War. Mitchell depicts the postwar Reconstruction years in Georgia as a desperate struggle to survive against great odds—against poverty and oppression, and

"Southerners who had turned Republicans very profitably—and carpetbaggers, these Yankees come south, like buzzards, after the surrender with all their worldly possessions in one carpet-bag."[23] The public and many literary critics applauded the book, responding enthusiastically to the engrossing story and deft characterizations. When producer David O. Selznick transformed Mitchell's romance of the Civil War and Reconstruction into a 220-minute Hollywood spectacular, film critics also received it warmly. Reflecting the received wisdom about Reconstruction, Frank S. Nugent wrote in *The New York Times:*

> Through stunning design, costume and peopling, Selznick's film has skillfully and absorbingly recreated Miss Mitchell's mural of the South in that bitter decade when secession, civil war, and reconstruction ripped wide the graceful fabric of the plantation age and confronted men and women who adorned it with the stern alternative of meeting the new era or dying with the old.[24]

So popular was the film that MGM re-released it for the movie theaters in 1954, 1961, 1967, 1978, 1989, and 1990 and once again in a restored version in 1998. The Turner Movie Classic television channel has also broadcast the film.

Revisionist fiction exists though it has had less success in overcoming the Reconstruction stereotype. Howard Fast (1914–2003), a Hollywood screenwriter and novelist, developed a Marxist-revisionist interpretation of Reconstruction reflecting the Du Bois approach in a vivid, passionate historical novel *Freedom Road* that has remained in print since 1944. In the story, the black hero Gideon Jackson, a member of the Charleston radical convention, finds support for his cause among "the poor white trash ... these despised scalawags, the tall, lean, slow spoken, straw haired men from the swamps and the lonely piney woods." But the alliance is short-lived. Through a combination of terrorism and racist appeals, the counterrevolutionary planters and their allies destroy the promise of democracy in the South. The final fantastic scene is a bloody *Gotterdamerung* as the freedmen and their poor white comrades fight to the death amid the ruins of a plantation home.[25] In his 1944 review for *The New York Times,* writer Bucklin Moon called it a

> fine and penetrating novel which differs in most respects from the popular conception of Northern carpetbaggers and Southern scalawags, freed slaves refusing to work until they received forty acres and a mule, and radical legislative bodies rushing toward anarchy and petty revenge for a beaten but still gallant South. Wrought out of the hopes and fears of the freed slave, and told with a simple dignity, it sets out to show that a workable democracy, which functioned for black and white alike, was betrayed by a planter group which would stop at nothing to bring back the autocracy of ante bellum days.[26]

It is a revisionist myth in counterpoint to the Dunning tradition. Yet, Fast believed otherwise. "I felt that I had written the truth," he commented. "I knew to my own satisfaction that it was the truth."[27]

WHISTLING DIXIE

Finally, let us note the persistence of the Reconstruction myth in song. On one neo-Confederate website you can find lyrics to a song attributed to a rebel major by the name of Innes Randolph. It is entitled "I'm a Good Ol' Rebel" (1914). "The end of the War brought the miseries of Reconstruction to the South," the editor states. "As burdensome as the struggle to adapt to life in the newly reconstituted Union was for most Southerners, it was a near impossibility for many an ex-Confederate soldier. The sentiments expressed in this classic post-war song were probably fairly typical among embittered veterans."

> I can't pick up my musket
> And fight 'um down no more
> But I ain't gonna love 'um

> Now that is certain sure
> And I don't want no pardon
> For what I was and am I won't be reconstructed
> And I do not give a damn.[28]

Fifty-five years later, in 1969, Robbie Robertson of the legendary rock group The Band, wrote "The Night They Drove Old Dixie Down"—a rebel lament about a fictional Southern soldier Virgil Cain. Along with "Dixie," you might call it the theme song of the Lost Cause ideology. (*Rolling Stone* magazine rated it as one of the top 500 songs of all time.) Here Robertson recalls the origins of the piece:

> When I first went down South, I remember that a quite common expression would be, "Well don't worry, the South's gonna rise again." At one point when I heard it I thought it was kind of a funny statement and then I heard it another time and I was really touched by it. I thought, "God, because I keep hearing this, there's pain here, there is a sadness here." In Americana land, it's a kind of a beautiful sadness.[29]

From that experience, he wrote:

> Like my father before me, I will work the land
> And like my brother above me, who took a rebel stand
> He was just eighteen, proud and brave,
> But a Yankee laid him in his grave.[30]

In addition, from the singer-songwriter Warren Zevon this lament for the South's Lost Cause in 1991:

> I've been a rebel all my days
>
> * * * *
>
> We were hopelessly outnumbered
> It was a lost cause all along
> But when we heard the bugles call
> We swore we'd stand or fall together right or wrong

We ain't seen no reconstruction here
Just the scorched earth all around
And the high school band played "Dixieland"
While they tore our tattered flags and banners down.[31]

In 2008, in another song, "Carpetbaggers," singer Jenny Lewis, with rock star Elvis Costello as backup, warned about gold-digging women in a metaphor that recalled the anti-Reconstruction image of the Yankee scoundrels who came south after the Civil War to exploit the Southern people:

They come to town when the war is over
Dirty boots in the middle of the night

* * * *

I'm a carpetbagger, baby
I'm coming to your town
I'm going to treat you kind (woo-hoo)
I'm going to rob you blind.[32]

HISTORY IN THE INTERROGATIVE MOOD

The long duration of wartime and postwar Reconstruction reflected the intractable issues that it attempted to address; the problems were labyrinthine in their complexity. The Civil War settled two things, as historian Bruce Catton noted: no state could leave the Union and slavery in America was dead.[33] Nevertheless, this left a great deal still to be decided—a list of truly unique and incredibly difficult questions. Here are some of the issues facing the nation in the 1860s and 1870s.

1. What was the legal status of the eleven defeated Confederate states? Was it simply a matter of "restoring" the rebel states to their former place in the Union? Did they retain all the rights and powers of a state within the United States constitutional system as if nothing had happened? Alternatively, did they exist in legal limbo? Did secession result in "state suicide"?

Had the Confederate states reverted to a kind of territorial status and therefore needed to apply for admission to the Union? On the other hand, in a variation on the territorial theory, were they now conquered "provinces" with no established rights at all, subject to the mercy of the victor? In other words, were they in the Union or out of the Union?

2. What should be done with the leaders of the failed rebellion? Should Jefferson Davis (the former President of the Confederate States of America) and Robert E. Lee (the Confederacy's most famous general), for example, be tried for treason? Should the secessionist lose their lands and civil rights?

3. Once slavery ended what would be the place in America for the 3,950,528 freedmen? What would freedom mean? How would they live? What role should the Federal government play in their transition from slavery to freedom? Should the ex-slaves have full citizenship and civil rights? Would black men vote and hold public office? What were their economic rights? What would be their relationship to their former masters and the non-slaveholding white Southerners? Should the Federal government confiscate rebel-owned plantations and turn the land over to the freedmen? What role would the freedmen themselves play in Reconstruction? (The questions about the present and future of the ex-slaves proved the most difficult of all.)

4. Who should define and control the process of Reconstruction? Was it the President's responsibility under the war powers granted to the executive branch by the Constitution? On the other hand, should Congress decide policy? What role would the Federal army of occupation play in the process?

5. On the domestic level, ordinary men and woman, former masters, former slaves, poor whites and yeomen farmers alike had to adjust to the social and economic changes brought on by war and emancipation. How would domestic life continue after the war? How had the experience of war affected the relationship between white Southern men and women? How would the veterans who had been absent for four years reassert their authority over the family and the

people they had once held as slaves? What did the women of the South, white and black, want in the new order of things? How would black families, separated during the slave years, reunite? What was the practical meaning of black liberation?

6. How would Southerners rebuild their economic infrastructure neglected or destroyed by the fighting—including the levees and the railroads? Who would provide the credit needed to rebuild the economy? How would taxes be paid and land restored to cultivation? (No one proposed a federal stimulus plan to rebuild the South.)

To complicate matters, the Constitution offered political leaders no clear or direct guidance or solutions. For its part, Washington provided no consistent guidance; plans continually changed, objectives defined and then redefined. The Republican politicians who dominated national politics were divided among themselves. They reflected a variety of personal and political persuasions (radical and moderate). Some wanted to restore the South to the Union without deep change. Others fought to remold the South into the image and likeness of a progressive, modernizing North. Northern Democrats, for their part, sided with their white conservative Southerners allies to resist even the most basic reforms.

As history played out there was no consistent approach or plan for answering these questions. Matters were complicated by racial prejudice (both in the North and the South), Southern intransience, confusion on the part of the South as to what exactly the North wanted them to do, and Lincoln's assassination fed the confusion. The result was a constant ebb and flow of objectives, plans, and schemes between 1861 and 1877.

THE CONTEST OVER RECONSTRUCTION

Historian James Oakes argues forcibly that the Republicans, despite their protestations before the war, were determined to abolish slavery. They would prevent its expansion and suck the oxygen out of the system—killing it over time. On the other hand, if the South left the Union in an attempt to protect slavery, the system would collapse under the weight of Union military might. Either way, the system was doomed.

The South decided on secession out of fear. The events of 1861–1865 validated their premonitions of the things to come. It was a fear that sooner or later, after Lincoln's election, the Republicans would move directly against the institution of slavery. Their anxieties were not exaggerated or unrealistic. One way or another, the North, as represented by the Lincoln administration, was determined, in relation to slavery, to reconstruct the South.

Why were white Southerners so agitated? Slavery was always two things to white Southerners. First, it was a system of labor, a way to get the cotton picked, the sugar cane cut, and the rice harvested. Second, and even more importantly, it was a system of race control. Virtually all white southerners believed in white supremacy, even those who owned no slaves at all. During the Civil War and Reconstruction, white Southerners were determined to preserve as much control over black labor as they could and, most important of all, preserve white supremacy.

Reconstruction was, in the early stages, a policy aimed at political reconciliation and the restoration of loyal state governments in the South yet consistent with Republican ideology. The process began in the first year of the war as soon as rebel territory came under Federal occupation. Lincoln believed that there remained a solid core of Southern unionists in the Confederate states following secession; secession, he argued, was the product of a conspiracy led by a minority of extremists. He counted on Union men to lead the South back into the Union. Lincoln also saw Reconstruction as an extension of the war effort. He was flexible and willing to make limited concessions and seek reconciliation but (and he was firm on this) without recognizing rebel independence, without allowing the expansion of slavery, and, importantly, without disavowing ultimate Republican goals. In the short term, the various designs for self-restoration of loyal state governments, put forth by Lincoln and others, illustrated the political and racial difficulties that would plague the Reconstruction process over the next four years of war and through twelve years of postwar strife. Perhaps Lincoln was moving toward a harder policy more in line with the designs of the Radicals, but his assassination altered the course of events.

The Republicans under Lincoln's astute political leadership had successfully concluded the Civil War, saved the Union, and moved slavery to the point of extinction. Republicans had won the presidency in 1860 and again in 1864. With Lincoln's death, the political situation changed dramatically: now a Southerner and a Democrat was in the White House. Radical Republicans initially saw Andrew Johnson as an ally. He had promised to "make treason odious" and he was anti-slavery. He proved, however, no friend of black rights and he held to a very strict interpretation of the Constitution. He was anti-slavery but *not* anti-South. He advocated for a quick restoration of the rebel states based on the idea that they had never left the Union. He and his supporters argued that he was only following in the footsteps of Lincoln. Johnson's plan of Reconstruction allowed the ex-rebel states to largely reconstruct themselves. As lawyer-historian Annette Gordon-Reed[34] wrote in her biography of Johnson:

> White southerners, who in the aftermath of Lincoln's death had waited in fear of what Johnson might do, were relieved and ecstatic about his [Johnson's] performance during the summer of 1865. Staunch Confederates hailed him as a hero and savior. Beyond the ending of slavery there would be no reformation of the southern racial landscape.

As a result, Hans L. Trefousse noted, the assassination of Lincoln removed a master politician and substituted "a man of narrow views about the Constitution and race for a statesman of far-reaching ability unhampered by ancient prejudices."[35] Johnson moved quickly to bring the rebel states back into the Union under a policy emphasizing pro-Southern restoration over Radical reformation. The result was an intense political and ideological battle between Johnson and the Republicans. Congress moved to take control of Reconstruction away from the president. In the end, the House of Representatives impeached Johnson. Although he was acquitted by the Senate, he emerged from the confrontation politically impotent. Nevertheless, Johnson's encouragement of Southern opposition to Reconstruction had the effect of delaying full civil rights for at least a hundred years as Gordon-Reed observes.

Despite Andrew Johnson's obstructionism Congress had already divided the former Confederacy into five military districts commanded by Federal generals. Now, the president was irrelevant with regard to any further Reconstruction policy. In truth, it was remarkable for its relative moderation. There was no round-up of political opponents, no show trials, no mass redistribution of property. Congressional policy, however, did represent a genuine attempt to create a bi-racial democracy in the South. Real gains were made: formal emancipation, public school systems, progressive state constitutions, black citizenship, and black voting. Additionally, Congress also sought to create a southern Republican party that would ensure that ex-rebels would not return to the Southern state houses or the halls of Congress. It is also remarkable that the freedmen did not advocate for revenge against their former masters or for the violent revolutionary change; they wanted education, the right to vote, and economic opportunity—a share in the American Dream (although the term was yet to be coined). Certainly, it was an American Tragedy that the white South could not look beyond race to see the potential benefits to both common whites and newly freed black people. Nevertheless, the white South from the beginning opposed the imposition of any "Radical Reconstruction." The political and paramilitary resistance of unreconstructed white Southerners to the agents of Reconstruction was, to use the term coined by British military historian John Keegan, an "informal secession."[36] Hardened by four years of conventional or guerilla warfare white Southerners engaged in a vicious insurgency that eventually wore down the Northern will to persist. Southerners thus "Redeemed" the South. The March 14, 1874 edition of *Harper's Weekly* ran a cartoon by Thomas Nast, America's greatest political cartoonist. The illustration is entitled "Colored Rule in a Reconstructed (?) State." The central figures in the cartoon are three grotesque black men in the South Carolina legislature. They engage in a violent argument calling one another thieves, liars, and rascals. The figure of Columbia presiding at the podium admonishes them: "You are aping the lowest whites. If you disgrace your race in this way you had better take back seats." Meanwhile, a white legislator holds his nose in contempt. Although Nast had been a strong supporter of the black vote and a critic of the Ku Klun Klan, his cartoon of 1874 illustrates the decline in the North for support for Reconstruction. So convincing was the ultimate Southern victory, that, with no great exaggeration, it can be argued that although the South may have lost the Civil War it "won" Reconstruction.

The issues of Reconstruction did not suddenly end with the Compromise of 1877. But the game was up; real power in the states of the former Confederacy had shifted to the conservative white "Redeemers." The full implications of their victory would not play out until the 1890s with the onset of the Age of Segregation and Disfranchisement. Now a new generation of whites, nursed on the teat of the Lost Cause, dominated the South. This "cause" was not in itself a political movement, but it provided the movement with an ideology. This victory was not only political and racial; the white South won control of the historical narrative as well. Historian Edward Ayers wrote:

> Most white Southerners never accepted the legitimacy of Reconstruction. They crushed black voting and other freedoms through violence, terrorism and fraud. When Reconstruction was driven from the South 12 years after it began, the white Southern majority rejoiced that true law, true justice, had returned. Confederate soldiers were lionized and a culture of defiance flourished. Over the next half-century the white South waged, and won, a propaganda war over the meaning of Reconstruction.[37]

"WHAT IS TRUTH?": HOLLYWOOD'S
RECONSTRUCTION

As propaganda, no single interpretation of the Civil War and Reconstruction had more influence on the American popular memory than *The Birth of a Nation*. In 1931, D. W. Griffith's epic silent film about the Civil War and Reconstruction reappeared in theaters in a re-edited version of the original movie of 1915. It now included a synchronized orchestral soundtrack, as well as sound effects. Additionally, a talking prelude introduced the film. In it actor Walter Huston interviewed Griffith about the origins and meaning of his creation. The two men, dressed in tuxedos, sit before a fireplace. Meanwhile, three young children secretly listen in the background, trying to "hear better" what the two grownups are saying:

Huston: Is it generally known that you are a Southerner?

Griffith: I should think it should be, it's been advertised enough. Yes, my father was a colonel in the Confederacy.
[As the conversation continues, Huston presents Griffith with a gift, "an old army sword worn by a Confederate officer."]

Griffith: Thank you, Walter. My father wore a sword like that.

Huston: When you made *The Birth of a Nation* did you tell your father's story?

Griffith: No, no. I didn't [pause] well, [he chuckles] now that you mention it perhaps I did.

Huston: How long did it take you?

Griffith: You ask me *more* questions. Oh, I suppose it began when I was a child. I used to get under a table and listen to my father and his friends talk about the battles they had been to and their struggles. Those things impress you deeply and I suppose those things go into *The Birth*.

Huston: You … ah … you feel as that it was true?

Griffith: Yes, I feel so, true as that blade. Oh, that's natural enough. You've heard your father tell about fighting day after day, night after night, and having nothing to eat but parched corn and your mother staying up nights [sewing] robes for the Klan. The Klan at that time was needed. It served a purpose. Yes, I think it was true. [Pause] So, as Pontius Pilate said. *"Truth?* What is the truth?"[38]

FILM AS EVENT, EXPERIENCE, AND MYTH

In trying to understand history, we are like those children off-screen once the conversation begins, trying to "hear better"—or like Griffith when he was a boy sitting under the table listening to old men's stories.

British novelist Virginia Woolf wrote:

> Is it not possible—I often wonder—that the things we have felt with such intensity have had an existence independent of our minds; are in fact still in existence? And if so, will it not be possible, in time, that some device will be invented by which we can tap them? Instead of remembering here a scene there a scene, I shall fit a plug into a wall; and listen to the past.[39]

Until then, what remains of past events is the evidence—always fragmentary and always subject to interpretation.

Historian Paul Cohen identifies three essential elements in how we understand the past: The historian *judges* that something important happened, *defines* the event, and *imposes a meaning* on that event and constructs a chronology. The past does not really exist until someone defines an event and gives it meaning. It is the historian's traditional or "familiar" role. It is often the stuff of textbooks, for example, that imply objectivity and "impartial storytelling." This is history as "event" or construction. History is also, Cohen observes, what people experience at the time. These are the witnesses to history—actors in a story but "blind" to the outcome. They do not know how the last act will turn out—they are "outcome blind." This is *history lived by the participants.* Their story comes to us in bits and pieces and is told to us later as a kind of recovered memory. Finally, we also understand *history as myth.* This is history used for some purpose—political, ideological, cultural, or racial. This is usable history or the past exploited for some "ulterior motive." Cohen argues that all three "pasts" contain truth and overlap in the narrative.[40]

We approach the event, experience, and myth of Reconstruction in film through essays intended to deepen our understanding of the postwar South: How were white Southerners able to control the narrative of Reconstruction history in contravention to the old adage that it is the "winners" who write history? What was the meaning and uses of the Myth of the Lost Cause? How would the history of Reconstruction have been different if Lincoln had lived? How did the war affect the lives of southern families, specifically women and children, both white and black? What was the extent and legacy of economic destruction in the South? What was the connection between wartime and postwar violence in the South? What price did black Southerners—the ex-slaves—pay for emancipation during and after the war? What were the consequences of the reconciliation of North and South after the end of Reconstruction? In answering these questions, we look at two ways in which the history is presented and understood—through the research of professional historians and through movies which, for the most part, replace history with myth. Each chapter will include a reflection of the topic in the movies—Hollywood's history of the Civil War and Reconstruction. In what ways did movies interpret the story? The films discussed in this book, either in detail or in brief, were selected to illustrate the way film has influenced thinking about the Civil War and Reconstruction. It is important to realize that films that we now regard as small, even trivial, contributed to a collective set of assumptions about the war and its aftermath. Obviously, *The Birth of a Nation* and *Gone with the Wind*—which are neither small nor trivial—must be considered to understand how movies interpreted the history of the Civil War and Reconstruction. Less obvious, but nevertheless true, the two Shirley Temple films discussed in the book—*The Littlest Rebel* and *The Little Colonel*—also provided a set of images and assumptions which, if not as powerful as those in *The Birth of a Nation* and *Gone with the Wind,* still helped to convince filmgoers that the myths, whether the "Moonlight and Magnolia" version or the "Plantation" version or the "Lost Cause" version, were grounded in reality.

2 Lincoln "Unmurdered"

Reconstruction Alternatives and Counterfactuals

10:10 PM. April 14, 1865. Ford's Theater, Washington, D.C. President and Mrs. Lincoln are in attendance. Major Henry Rathbone with his fiancée Clara Harris, a young friend of Mrs. Lincoln, has accompanied the President and First Lady to see *Our American Cousin,* a popular comedy about a rustic American (Asa Trenchard) among English aristocrats. Act III, Scene II.

Mrs. Mountchessington:	I am aware, Mr. Trenchard, you are not used to the manners of good society, and that, alone, will excuse the impertinence of which you have been guilty.
Asa Trenchard:	Don't know the manners of good society, eh? Well, I guess I know enough to turn you inside out, old gal—you sockdologizing old man-trap. (The audience erupts in laughter.)

At that moment, John Wilkes Booth opens the door to the box where the presidential party is sitting. He points a "Philadelphia Derringer" at the back of the President's head. Rathbone turns, sees the weapon and, acting quickly, hits Booth's arm. The tiny pistol discharges but misses its mark. A brief struggle ensues and Rathbone is seriously wounded when Booth draws a dagger from his belt and stabs him in the arm. But Lincoln, still strong despite the rapid aging so evident in his last photograph, grabs Booth in a bear hug from behind, throws the would-be assassin to the floor and sits on him until others drag him away. The President is safe. Mary Lincoln has fainted. The next day a front-page column in *The New York Times* begins:

Attempted Assassination of Lincoln
President Still Alive
The Act of a Desperate Rebel

That afternoon, Lincoln tells Secretary of War Edwin M. Stanton one of his "stories"—something about a Sangamon county farmer who tried to put an old, swayback nag out of its misery but misses and shoots himself in the foot. He laughs at his own joke; Stanton is not amused.

IF LINCOLN HAD LIVED

We know, of course, that Lincoln was murdered by John Wilkes Booth. But it did not have to come out that way: "What if Lincoln had lived?" Answering the question brings us into the realm of alternative or counterfactual history. Consider three approaches to answering the question. The first is to dismiss it. In a famous essay entitled *What Is History?* British historian E.H. Carr, who had very strong opinions about what historians should do and not do, argued that "historians in practice do not assume that events are inevitable before they have taken place. They frequently discuss alternative courses available to the actors in the story on the assumption that the option was open." And, "as a historian," he states, he is "perfectly prepared to do without" the "inevitable," the "unavoidable," the "inescapable" or the "ineluctable." Certainly, "life would be drabber" without alternatives. "But," he concludes, "let us leave them to poets and metaphysicians."[1] The second approach is limited only by the imagination of a poet, a metaphysician, or in the case of Harry Turtledove, a novelist. In *The Guns of the South,* he provides a fantastic alternative to the outcome of the American Civil War.[2] The cover illustrates the book's conceit: It shows General Robert E. Lee holding a twentieth-century Russian-made assault rifle— an AK-47. The South wins the Civil War when white South Africans, intent on changing the course of world history in favor of white supremacy, invent a time machine that allows the government to transport a team of military advisors from 2014 back in time to 1863 and the battlefield at Gettysburg. Robert E. Lee is the hero of the novel and he, in the complex "history" in the novel, is actually instrumental in freeing the slaves after the war. Lincoln survives the war, but surrenders himself to Lee. As fascinating as this premise might be, this is the realm of science fiction, "clever curiosities and flights of imagination," not the realm of the possible.[3] The third approach to alternative or counterfactual history, what we examine in this chapter, is implicit in the historical craft and is limited to speculation or the imagination within "the horizon of possibility." André Maurois, the French novelist, biographer, and historian, argued that "There is no privileged past"; rather, "There is an infinitude of Pasts, all equally as valid … At each and every instant of Time, however brief you suppose it, the line of events forks like a stem of a tree putting forth twin branches."[4] In other words, the third approach is a principled argument against causal determinism.[5] In this case, the question ("What if Lincoln had lived?") requires no science-fiction time machine to answer and, despite what E. H. Carr says, is inherent in the historian's craft. Regarding Lincoln's assassination and the history of Reconstruction, for example, historian Ward M. McAfee states that "In the crafting of historical literature, facts rarely speak for themselves. Conjecture often shapes written history at least as much as hard evidence."[6]

Consider historian Roger L. Ransom's *The Confederate States of America: What Might Have Been* (2005). Written as a counterfactual history of the rebel states, it cites real sources and includes all the paraphernalia of legitimate historical investigation—a discussion of the historiography of the Civil War and postwar years, endnotes, and an extensive bibliography. Nothing is all that fantastic here; Ransom describes what happened as well as what might have happened. He is writing serious history and takes "What if?" seriously as well. In his story, Lincoln is defeated for reelection in 1864 by a Democrat—Horatio Seymour. Lincoln lives but is out of power and slavery lives on too until its demise in 1880. Ransom deepens our understanding of what really happened during the Civil War and postwar years by asking legitimate questions about choices that Americans faced at the time. So, what if Lincoln had lived either because Booth missed his shot or because of some other twist of fate?

Questions about the consequences of Lincoln's death, in fact, were asked in 1865 by people North and South and afterwards by a variety of commentators and historians. Southerners, for their part, reacted to the news of Lincoln's death in various ways. Many rejoiced. Others kept their opinions to themselves if they lived in areas occupied by Union troops or made a show of mourning to avoid Yankee vengeance. Others were concerned that the death of Lincoln was not a good thing for the South. In Galveston, Texas, William Pitt Ballinger, a prominent attorney, wrote: "The future I confess looks to me all gloom and darkness, Lincoln was a kindly man ... Lincoln would have been content to restore the Union and anxious to conciliate and reconcile the South ..."[7]. In other words, Ballinger believed that the postwar years would have been different with Lincoln "unmurdered." He was not the only one who speculated on an alternative history and postulated a postwar American free of the oppression and corruption of the Reconstruction years in line with the Lost Cause myths of the Civil War and its aftermath. If only Lincoln had lived. As Ward McAfee puts it regarding Lincoln's last days in office, the issue of counterfactual history in the case of Lincoln and Reconstruction "cannot be avoided."[8] Here are two alternatives regarding the Reconstruction years: (1) Lincoln lives and continues a moderate policy of "restoration" of loyal state governments in the South without "reconstruction," ensuring only the future loyalty of the ex-rebels and emancipation; or (2) Lincoln lives but moves closer to the Radicals through a policy of genuine reconstruction in response to the South's dogged determination to restore the old social and political order at the expense of true Southern unionists and the rights of the freedmen. It is the former interpretation that has dominated the narrative of Reconstruction.

LINCOLN THE MERCIFUL

The image of Lincoln the Merciful, who, if he had lived, would have enforced no hard or vengeful peace has been the subject of both Hollywood films and historical speculation. It is also central to the myth of the Lost Cause. But the assertion of Lincoln's greatness and magnanimity, as president and beyond that as a near deity, took some time to come into focus. Melvyn Stokes, in his detailed analysis of *The Birth of a Nation,* quotes historian Eric F. Goldman on the immediate aftermath of Lincoln's assassination: "Although the subject [at the time of his death] of a great deal of immediate sentimentality, [he] did not become the unassailable Abraham Lincoln of the schoolbooks until two decades after his murder." Stokes indicates that the "towering genius" and humanitarian came into existence in the 1880s and 1890s, first with the 1890 publication of the ten-volume *Abraham Lincoln: A History* by John G. Nicolay and John Hay, which had been serialized in *The Century* magazine in the 1880s. In contrast, in 1889 Lincoln's former law partner William Henry Herndon (with Jesse William Weik) had published a critical and debunking view of Lincoln (*Herndon's Lincoln: the True Story of a Great Life … The History and Personal Recollections of Abraham Lincoln by William Henry Herndon*). By the time of publication of the book, however, the attack on the "now-expanding" Lincoln myth did not attract many readers, and his book was either reviled, or perhaps worse, ignored.

Moreover, the work on Lincoln by Ida M. Tarbell, starting in November, 1897 in *McClure's Magazine* went a long way toward solidifying the heroic image of Lincoln. Where Herndon had portrayed Lincoln as a *Westerner,* "plain, frank, and at times crude, Tarbell had presented him as a great man not so much *despite* his background as *because* of it. In essence Tarbell created a folk myth of Lincoln as the conscious descendent of generations of pioneers."[9] Thus, through the efforts of Tarbell and many others, the popular image of Lincoln that we now take for granted came into being.

By historical coincidence, the consequences of which no one could have foreseen or even imagined, as the Lincoln image took shape in print in the last half of the 1890s, a new and even more powerful tool for not only creating images but also spreading them far beyond what print could achieve emerged, namely the invention of the movies. Out of the many portrayals of Lincoln that began almost immediately in movies, the most common was the "humane and merciful Lincoln,"[10] the epitome of which is a scene in *The Birth of a Nation* (a description of this scene will appear later in this chapter).

Bruce Chadwick, in his invaluable *The Reel Civil War: Myth-making in American Film,* indicates that Lincoln "has appeared as a least a minor character in more than 150 films and another 50 made-for-television movies or television specials or series— more than any other American figure."[11] Chadwick also estimates that there have been 500 silent and over 200 sound films that deal with the Civil War.

Chadwick shows that "humane and merciful Lincoln" is, in many cases, also a "doddering old man," with Lincoln constantly weeping and seen praying for the end of the war (and not only that but also frequently seen wearing a shawl like some aged grandmother). The "real" Lincoln, the masterful politician, is nowhere to be seen. On this issue, Chadwick is worth quoting at length:

> In film after film, from the early years of the silents through made for television films of the 1990s, Lincoln was routinely seen as a gentle giant, a towering emancipator in black suit, shawl and stovepipe hat: Father Abraham. In most, he was seen pardoning Northern and Southern soldiers, being kind to children, urging reconciliation in meetings in parlors, walking slowly towards some heavenly light up ahead and, quite often, being murdered in Ford's Theatre. America was spoon-fed a combination father-favorite uncle, beloved minister-schoolteacher, a loving religious Lincoln, a political figure who embodied the best of humankind, a soothing

figure somehow removed from both space and time, the universal President ... He was the single greatest catalyst in reunion movies, and the myths created about him on the screen were the strongest evidence and best examples of the power of celluloid mythmakers.[12]

The image(s) of Lincoln as "catalyst" for "reunion" is a key concept, epitomized in *The Birth of a Nation* by Lincoln's plan *not* to treat the South as a conquered enemy when the war ends. He rejects Austin Stoneman's (Thaddeus Stevens, a Radical Republican and the powerful chair of the House Ways and Means Committee) demand for punishment and declares, via title card, that he will deal with the seceded states "as though they had never been away."[13] Later, after Lincoln has been assassinated, Dr. Cameron (a courtly Southern patriarch) cries out: "Our best friend is gone. What is to become of us now?" The comments by Lincoln himself and by Dr. Cameron in *The Birth of a Nation* rehearse the theme, especially in the South, of Lincoln as the soul of reunion. As Chadwick notes:

> The Lincoln legend grew in the South, too. Lincoln's death in 1865 brought on [a hard] Reconstruction and with it a certain feeling in Dixie that if Lincoln had lived, his Reconstruction plan, softer on the South would have helped reunite the nation. In death, Lincoln, reviled in the South throughout the war, surprisingly became an acceptable Southern hero of sorts.

And this "redesigned" Lincoln "was the next logical step in the reconstruction of Civil War history."[14] The "redesigned" Lincoln was a surprising aspect of the "Lost Cause" mythology, part of the disastrous and pernicious distortion of Civil War history. Part of Griffith's sentimentality towards Lincoln perhaps also stemmed from the fact that in 1898, as a young actor, "Griffith scored a personal triumph with his depiction of Abraham Lincoln in William Haworth's play *The Ensign*."[15]

As Stokes and Chadwick indicate, Lincoln was depicted in silent films almost from the very beginning of narrative cinema. Stokes mentions films such as *The Reprieve* (1908), *Abraham Lincoln's Clemency* (1910), *One Flag at Last* (1911), *When Lincoln Was President* (1913), and *The Songbird of the North* (1913) as depicting the "humane and merciful" Lincoln. Stokes observes:

> Maybe the most fanciful of all these films was *The Toll of War* (1913), in which Lincoln freed a Southern girl sentenced to death for spying against the North. After her release, she saw the assassination of Lincoln at Ford's Theatre. The President was carried to her nearby room and died in her bed while she knelt beside him in prayer.[16]

The description of Lincoln as "the Great Heart" of course comes from *The Birth of a Nation,* although, as Stokes points out:

> The first overt mention of the war comes with the first tableau in the film: a facsimile of Lincoln signing the first call for 75,000 volunteers ... In reality, of course, the first act in the conflict had been the Confederate firing on Fort Sumter on April 12, 1861. To have mentioned this, however, would have made it clear that the South, far from being a victim, was the real aggressor in the conflict.[17]

In essence, Lincoln, driven by the "irrational" abolitionists such as Austin Stoneman, seals the fate of the South which embodied, as an early title card puts it, the "quaint life that is no more." Nevertheless, by also depicting Lincoln as *weeping* and *praying* as he signs the proclamation, the image of the "humane and merciful" Lincoln comes into being.

In one scene in *The Birth of a Nation,* Ben Cameron, "the Little Colonel" and the epitome of the Confederate Cavalier, lies in a union hospital recovering from his wounds. On the battlefield, his courage, of course, had been magnificent; he even had time to pause and offer water to a badly wounded Union soldier, an act that provoked cheers from both Southern *and* Northern troops. A title card reveals that a "secret influence" has declared Cameron to be a guerrilla and thus must be hanged. Cameron's mother and Elsie Stoneman, who are both visiting him, decide their only hope is Abraham Lincoln. Cameron's mother declares, "We will ask mercy from the Great Heart." Looking old, weary, and on the verge of tears (again), Lincoln pardons Cameron and his mother returns to the hospital to tell him, "Mr. Lincoln has given back your life to me."

Shortly thereafter Lee surrenders at Appomattox. A title card declares that Lee's surrender means "the end of state sovereignty." A dispirited and shabby Ben Cameron returns to what's left of his home and family. Meanwhile Radicals demand that Lincoln hang the Southern leaders and treat the Southern states as conquered provinces. Lincoln, as mentioned above, declares he will deal with the South as if it had never been away. No wonder, then, that Dr. Cameron, as also mentioned above, declares after Lincoln is assassinated: "Our best friend is gone. What is to become of us now?" One curious feature of Griffith's Lincoln, however, as Robert Lang notes, is his strangely "androgynous" quality, as Lincoln "combines masculine *and* feminine qualities. He is a bearded man, but he is sensitive to his own feelings and those of others. He is ready to make war on the South, but he cries after signing the proclamation calling for volunteers. He angrily dismisses the man speaking to him before his meeting with Elsie and Mrs. Cameron, but finally gives in to the emotional persuasions of the Little Colonel's mother to save her son's life. In the last moments before he is shot, Lincoln draws a shawl around his shoulders, perhaps symbolizing his awareness of the chill of his impending death ... As a gesture, however ... it is "coded culturally as feminine." In *The Birth of a Nation,* Lincoln is both a father *and* mother to his people.[18]

THE LITTLEST REBEL MEETS THE MERCIFUL LINCOLN

The pernicious legacy of *The Birth of a Nation* paved the way, twenty years later, for the "benevolently" racist *The Littlest Rebel* (1935), which brought another visit to Lincoln by two petitioners seeking a pardon from "the Great Heart." But here Ben Cameron ("little Colonel") has been replaced by the "littlest rebel" in the person of seven-year-old Shirley Temple, the greatest child star in film history. She is "Virgie" (Virginia), daughter of yet another Cavalier gentleman of the old South. He goes to war but sneaks back from time to time, through Union lines, to visit Virgie and his wife. But before he leaves, the movie comments on whether slavery is the cause of the Civil War. In line with the part of the Lost Cause myth that no one, except meddling abolitionists, caused the war, certainly no one in the South, this exchange takes place between Virgie and "Uncle Billy" as her father prepares to march off to war:

Uncle Billy:	No one knows why there will be a war. There's a man up north who wants to free the slaves.
Virgie:	What does that mean?
Uncle Billy:	I don't know myself.

His last visit corresponds to the death of his wife and, with the help of a sympathetic Union officer (who even lends the father his uniform), he tries to make it through the lines to get Virgie safely to Richmond. They are caught, however, and both he and the Union officer are sentenced to death. Yet another sympathetic Union officer—Virgie's charm and shining personality overwhelm everyone who meets her—gives Virgie and her devoted (former) slave "Uncle Billy" enough money (she and "Uncle Billy" haven't quite made enough with their song-and-dance fundraiser renditions of "Polly Wolly Doodle") to travel to Washington where "the Great Heart" appears to have very little to do except listen to pleas for clemency. Lincoln welcomes them into his office, even shaking hands with "Uncle Billy," who reacts in amazement. He sits at his desk, puts Virgie on his lap, peels an apple which he shares with her and, after a brief exchange where Virgie's charm makes his heart even greater, issues a pardon to both her father and the Union officer. In the last scene, at the prison, just before the two men are released, Virgie and "Uncle Billy" sing and dance "Polly Wolly Doodle" for a combined audience of appreciative Union guards and Confederate prisoners.

Chadwick concludes:

> World War I ended the first era of Civil War movies and World War II ended the second, and the Lincoln movies as well. The sixteenth president quickly disappeared from the nation's movie screens when World War II began. Whatever romantic notions about the Civil War and Lincoln film had conjured up prior to 1941 were immediately washed away by the grim reality of the latest war.[19]

Lincoln continued to make occasional appearances in films of the 1940s and beyond. In 1930, D.W. Griffith himself directed *Abraham Lincoln,* which he hoped would be a masterpiece but came out as something much less. *Young Mr. Lincoln* (1939) and *Abe Lincoln in Illinois* (1940) were far more critically successful. After 1940, the depiction of Lincoln in film (and later television) declined into random minor appearances. One exception was the five-part program *Mr. Lincoln* (1952/53) presented on the *Omnibus* television series. The actor who played Lincoln—Royal Dano—later became the voice of Lincoln in the Disneyland and Disneyworld audio-animatronic Lincoln in the "Great Moments with Mr. Lincoln" and in the Hall of Presidents. In the 2005 mock documentary *C.S.A.: The Confederate States of America,* which posits a south victorious in the Civil War, Lincoln flees Washington but is captured in blackface make-up.

"LONESOMEST JOB IN THE WORLD": *TENNESSEE JOHNSON*

Tennessee Johnson (1942) is about Lincoln's Vice President, Andrew Johnson, suddenly elevated to become the 17th President as a result of Lincoln's murder. Directed by Hollywood veteran William Dieterle and written by the quartet of Milton Ginzberg, Alvin Meyers, John Balderston, and Wells Root, it features Van Heflin as Johnson, Ruth Hussy as his wife—Eliza McCardle Johnson—and Lionel Barrymore as Johnson's nemesis Thaddeus Stevens. The film follows Johnson from his youth as an illiterate drifter to his impeachment trial in the Senate. By being generous, one could describe the film as "somewhat historically inaccurate," especially the film's climatic scene where Johnson enters the Senate chamber, near the end of the trial, to deliver a stirring speech in his own defense. One could point out that Johnson never appeared in the Senate chamber to defend himself, that in fact he was represented throughout by legal counsel. But even generosity has its limits; historical inaccuracies abound. The film begins with a crawl announcing that in 1867 a law was passed making the firing of cabinet members unconstitutional. Since the film reveals that Johnson opposed that law, the crawl concludes by "vindicating" Johnson with a statement that the Supreme Court overturned the law in 1926.

The film begins in 1830 when Johnson—a runaway from being bound to a tailor in "Carolina"—decides to settle in Tennessee and support himself mending clothes. Admitting that he can't read, he asks the town librarian (who will obviously become his wife) to teach him. He quickly educates himself in law and politics and sees himself as the voice of the property-less "white trash" as he calls himself and is persuaded to take up the cause of voting rights for the common man. Everything in the Declaration of Independence, the Constitution, and the Bill of Rights applies to him and his kind, he declares. They are "the people." Of course, the propertied classes close ranks against such talk. The local sheriff makes it clear: "the man who owns the country should run it."

Despite violence directed against Johnson and his supporters, he refuses to answer with violence, maintaining his beliefs in "laws" and "rights." Not surprisingly, in all these events—in ante-bellum Tennessee!—not a single African American is seen in any capacity, slave or free. Once Johnson's integrity and nobility have been established, the film simply leaps ahead to 1860. Johnson is now a pro-Union Democratic senator from Tennessee. When Jefferson Davis calls on all Southern senators to leave the

Union, Johnson refuses and is branded a "traitor" by the secessionist Senators. Johnson serves in the Union army and "saves" Nashville from a Confederate Army takeover. The 1864 convention initiates the later conflicts between Johnson and Stevens. Lincoln opposes Stevens' party plank that the South must be punished after the war. Johnson agrees, favoring reconciliation (the magic world finally surfaces). Despite their intense disagreement, Stevens does not oppose Lincoln selecting Johnson as his running mate in the election. At the inauguration, a very ill Johnson makes a speech but appears to be drunk. Despite widespread condemnation and ridicule, Lincoln writes Johnson a letter of support asking Johnson to help "patch up the torn garment of our nation."

As the war ends, John Wilkes Booth tries to visit Johnson who, meanwhile, tells his wife that the war's end will "start an era of good feeling." As Johnson speaks to a crowd, quoting Lincoln on "binding up the nation's wounds," Lincoln is assassinated. The new President now sees himself in the "lonesomest job in the world" constantly asking himself, "what would Lincoln have done?" and groaning, "I am not fit to follow him."

Johnson is immediately challenged by Thaddeus Stevens and the vengeance-crazed Radical Republicans who no longer have the brilliant and humane Lincoln to keep them in check. A delegation tells Johnson to "treat the South as an outside conquered nation," demanding that each "colored man" be given forty acres and a mule. Johnson rejects the idea, claiming that Lincoln had asserted that the Southern states were "never" out of the Union. Stevens and his crew storm off while threatening impeachment. And impeachment eventually comes. Johnson, who claims that he was carrying out Lincoln's plan for reconciliation and reunification, repeatedly clashes with the angry and frustrated Radicals. Johnson fires a cabinet member in violation of the "law" (Tenure of Office Act) passed by the Radicals. Johnson declares he will "pardon" all "former masters" and restore citizenship to all who fought for the "lost cause" of the Confederacy. Stevens argues that every rebel snake in the South will crawl into the daylight; that Johnson is starting a "new civil war"; and that Johnson apparently has no sympathy for the four million former slaves. One could say—ironically, if the irony of all this was not so tragic—that Stevens was absolutely right as to what would be the consequences of Johnson's idea of reconciliation. Johnson argues that he wants "all races" to live together peacefully; that Stevens's ideas would make slaves of whites; and that Stevens has the drive of a "great fanatic." Thus the film makes clear who is to be regarded as right and who wrong in this titanic argument.

Johnson is impeached by a vengeful House and the Senate trial begins. In a truly revealing moment when the filmmakers apparently could not see what was right in front of them, Stevens, now very ill and unable to walk, is *carried into the Senate chamber by two young African Americans.*

In his own defense, although contrary to the actual trial, Johnson enters the Senate where he is met by boos and jeers; even the Chief Justice, presiding at the trial, has difficulty restoring order. Stevens is certain that Johnson will make another "drunken" speech and ensure his conviction and removal from the presidency. Johnson reads Lincoln's earlier letter, supporting him against the charges of being drunk. He claims that his impeachment is not for any "crimes" but for "reaching out" to the South. He points at the twenty empty desks in the Senate chamber and asks why haven't the twenty Southern senators who once occupied them been restored to their positions. He accuses Stevens and his followers of continuing the war. While those desks remain empty, he proclaims, there is no Union and throws in a warning about "foreign" threats to the country if reconciliation fails.

At the vote, Senator Huyler, a "sure" vote against Johnson first faints and then votes "not guilty." Johnson, reconciliation, the Union, the myth of the "Lost Cause" all survive. Of course, the four million recently freed slaves from the story disappear at the end of Reconstruction and the onset of Jim Crow.

The film ends with Grant's presidency. Johnson has been returned to the Senate by the voters of Tennessee. He is now applauded by all as he speaks of the vacant desks no longer vacant, of the fact that the South is back in the Union. This is what

Abraham Lincoln lived, fought, and died for, the Union of these states, one and inseparable, now and forever. Thus the myths lived on in 1942, unchallenged and overpowering. The United States was now at war with Germany, Italy, and Japan. The idea of a "united" and reconciled country could accept no historical "truth" about the meaning of reunion opposing the seventy years of entrenched distortions.

HISTORIANS AND "THE GREAT HEART"

In 1935, Lloyd Lewis—journalist, raconteur, biographer of Grant and Sherman, and Lincoln scholar—speculated in a speech at the University of Chicago on "the course of American life" if Lincoln had lived. He asked his audience to "suppose, if you will, that Mr. Lincoln had not been murdered at all, and had lived out his allotted span of life—or at least his second term in the Presidency." Would Honest Abe have gone down to defeat, into impeachment, and political disgrace like Andrew Johnson? Would Lincoln, like Johnson, have failed to carry out "something sensible, tolerant, and fair to the conquered South"? Would Lincoln "unmurdered" have failed as Johnson failed? Johnson, according to the traditional view of Reconstruction, had been "crucified" by vindictive Radical Republicans intent on black rule and on punishing the South for the crime of secession. But President Johnson was too honest, too decent to support such actions. Rather than administer an unjust peace he went down "to exhausted political defeat." Lincoln was also too kind, too forgiving. Thus, it was better that Lincoln was assassinated—his reputation still intact. "Lincoln died just in time," the traditionalists said. Such was the commonly accepted historical view of Lincoln and Reconstruction when Lewis spoke. Lincoln was too good hearted to face down the Radicals. This is also the image of Lincoln in *The Birth of a Nation:* "the Great Heart." Ridiculous, Lewis stated. This was folk memory of the "religio-romantic" sort. While Johnson was "obtuse, stubborn, and blundering," Lincoln was "resourceful, sagacious, and diplomatic." He was a skilled politician of the highest order. We have, Lewis said, overestimated the "goodness of his heart" and underestimated Lincoln's shrewdness. Lincoln was no sentimental fool. Consider Lincoln's performance during the war. Are you telling me, Lewis asked, that a man who proved "more than a match for Jefferson Davis and Robert E. Lee ... could not have hoped to match himself against Charles Sumner, Thad Stevens, and Ben Wade ..."? Lincoln was a political actor of great talent and postwar politics dominated the second act of the drama of the Civil War. Lincoln had outsmarted the South militarily and politically. He had maneuvered the South into firing the first shot, convinced the slave owners of the Border States to support the Union, and prevented Great Britain from intervening in the conflict. Topping this, Lincoln had been reelected to the presidency, had freed the slaves, and had saved the Union. War was the hard part. Peace by comparison would be easy.

Lewis, however, was still in the traditionalists' camp when it came to interpreting "Black Reconstruction." The South, he asserted, was willing to meet Lincoln halfway and Southerners were convinced that Lincoln would not impose black rule over white people. Lincoln was essentially conservative and looked to conservative white Southerners to restore the South to the Union: They knew Lincoln as the hope of the South.

As for the Radical Republicans, they were only a faction within the Republican Party, their political base limited to reformist New England and New York. Lincoln had only to rally the agrarian West, Northern farmers, and the legions of still serving Union soldiers and their discharged comrades. The Army, he asserted, was loyal to their old Commander in Chief. Further, their commanding generals were mostly Democrats who opposed "Negro rule." The Army would be the critical swing vote in the state and Congressional elections of 1865 and 1866. The Radical Republicans could not hold against such an alliance. As the head of a true "Union Party," Lincoln would have insisted on a conservative restoration of the South led by Southern planters and supported by conservative Northern allies. And Lincoln, "unmurdered," guided the nation until 1868: a wise, conservative, hero of the masses. No carpetbaggers. No scalawags. No black rule. The nation was "happier." Such was Lloyd Lewis's alternative history.[20] There are, however, other theories, other counterfactual speculations.

This much we know for sure. Lincoln believed that the majority of the Southern people were Unionist at heart and that secession had been brought on by disloyal men who misled the mass of common men in the South who were essentially loyal. He hoped that Southern loyalists could effect a quick reunion with limited black suffrage. Lincoln's plan of reconstruction, however, faced strong opposition from the Radical Republicans. This Lincoln could not ignore. Also, Lincoln did not see the Radicals as enemies; he could work with them. They opposed a mere restoration of the Southern states without real reform and a strong commitment to black rights. In fact, Lincoln by 1865 had moved, or evolved, in his position on black rights and the need to take a harder line with the South. He could work with the Radicals. Lewis was right in this—the President was master of politics and expert at manipulating his political opponents— but wrong perhaps as to how he would have used those talents.

So, consider these alternatives offered by today's Civil War historians: "It was once assumed," historian George Rable says, "that Lincoln, had he lived, would have taken a much more conservative course toward Reconstruction than the path favored by the Radicals and many moderate Republicans." Lincoln was conservative but, he contends, Lincoln "would not have broken with the Republicans as Johnson did." Craig Symonds, for his part, judges that

> Lincoln knew how far he could go and where he could not go. Lincoln believed blacks should have citizenship and the right to vote. He knew how far and how fast he could go. Lincoln would have pursued the goals of the Radicals with a velvet glove.

But this assumes that the South would have cooperated with Lincoln.

For his part, Gerald Prokopowicz offers this counterfactual: It was Lincoln's assassination alone "that made him into a national icon." If he had lived "we would have no Lincoln Memorial, no Lincoln penny, no Lincoln on Mont Rushmore." He reminds us that this president "was controversial and in some quarters very unpopular …"[21] Mark Grimsley, also believes that Lincoln would have had a very difficult time with Reconstruction despite his remarkable political skills. The only way Reconstruction could be a success was to ensure black rights, including the unrestricted right to vote. But white Southerners were consistently and violently opposed to this. Also, consider this: Even if Lincoln had sided fully with the Radical agenda he would have failed to force a lasting Radical Reconstruction when you take into account the sullen, hostile white population in the Southern states. Lincoln underestimated Unionist feelings in the South. In the South race always trumped unionism. Lincoln's plan of Reconstruction was essentially a plan for Southerners to reconstruct themselves. Today we know how Reconstruction turned out after fifteen years of political opposition and violent resistance in the states of the former Confederacy.

It is inconceivable that Lincoln would have made the political mistakes that Andrew Johnson made; but that does not mean that Lincoln's policies, tentative and largely unformed in 1865, would have worked. Counterfactual or alternative history requires that the alternative story have a large measure of plausibility. By 1877, after years of political and violent resistance, reactionary Southern insurgents were in control of the South. The South may have lost the war but it is not an exaggeration to say that the South won Reconstruction. Even under "the Great Heart," it would have taken a Second Reconstruction a hundred years later to begin meaningful social, political, and economic change in the states of the former Confederacy. What was the possibility that had Lincoln lived Reconstruction would have turned out differently?

Steven Spielberg's film *Lincoln* (2012) has the president convincing Radical Republican Thaddeus Stevens that he must control his radicalism so as not to alienate conservatives and moderates in the House of Representatives whose votes were necessary to move forward on the passage of a thirteenth amendment outlawing slavery. This is Spielberg's version of "the Great Heart." Film critic Anthony Lane, writing in the *New Yorker* magazine, observed:

> We have a John Williams score (for the film) all plaintive piano solos and sobbing horns, that could have been composed thirty years ago. In the same vein, our first sight of Lincoln is from behind, the radiance of his fame being too much to contemplate head on, and we even get a foolish coda, with our hero manifested like an angel through a flickering candle flame.[22]

Later, in a private conversation with Stevens in the movie, it is clear that Lincoln wants forgiveness toward the South and a go-slow policy regarding Reconstruction:

Lincoln [Daniel Day-Lewis]:	I can't ensure a single damn thing if you scare the whole House with talk of land appropriations and revolutionary tribunals and punitive thisses and thats—
Thaddeus Stevens [Tommy Lee Jones]:	When the war ends, I intend to push for full equality, the Negro vote and much more. Congress shall mandate the seizure of every foot of rebel land and every dollar of their property. We'll use their confiscated wealth to establish hundreds of thousands of free Negro farmers, and at their side soldiers armed to occupy and transform the heritage of traitors. We'll build up a land down there of free men and free women and free children and freedom. The nation needs to know that we have such plans.
Lincoln:	That's the untempered version of reconstruction. It's not ... It's *not exactly* what I intend, but we shall oppose one another in the course of time. Now we're working together, and I'm asking you—

Thaddeus Stevens:	For patience, I expect.
Lincoln:	When the people disagree, bringing them together requires going slow till they're ready to make up—

The dialogue is fictional; no one recorded this private conversation between Lincoln and Stevens. Nevertheless, the screenwriter, Tony Kushner, imagined what they said based on the idea that Lincoln wanted a merciful ending to the war. He, of course, is not alone in believing that had "the Great Heart" continued to beat, the story of Reconstruction would have turned out differently—not only Lincoln unmurdered but the Southern people unpunished.

So, what would have happened if Lincoln had lived? In his speech on Reconstruction on April 11, 1865, three days before that tragic evening at the theater, Lincoln stated that he was open to compromise on Reconstruction policy and conscious of the difficulties of putting the pieces of the nation back together again: "We simply must begin with, and mold [policy] from, disorganized and discordant elements." He understood that the cooperation of Southern white people was the key element in Reconstruction—what he defined as the "re-inauguration of the national authority ..." His was a "practical" plan open to revision and compromise. "It may be my duty to make some new announcement to the people of the South," he said regarding Reconstruction.[23] But Lincoln himself had doubts that his own scheme to restore the Union would work and to the degree that the federal government could intervene in the Southern states. "We can't take to running state governments in all of these southern states," he conceded during a cabinet meeting in 1865. "Their people must do that, although I recon at first, they may do it badly." Indeed, they did do it badly. And Congress, in the face of Johnson's intransigency and the obstinacy of the ex-Confederates, took full control of the process out of the president's hands. They instituted a "radical" Reconstruction that was, in truth, a hard but not oppressive plan to reform the South. Lincoln, had he lived and in concert with the Radicals, may very well have done the same. It is inconceivable that having led the nation in a bloody war to preserve the Union and, yes, to free the slaves, he would have allowed all that work to be undermined by the former Confederates. It is true that there are many examples of Lincoln's humanity and mercy. Spielberg again:

Lincoln
Now, here's a sixteen year old boy. They're going
to hang him …

(Hay startles awake, then settles. He's used to this. Lincoln reads a little further.)

He was with the 15th Indiana Calvary near Beaufort,
seems he lamed his horse to avoid battle.

I don't think even Stanton would complain if I pardoned him?
You think Stanton would complain?

(Nicolay stirs in the next bed.)

John Hay
Ummm … I don't know, sir, I don't know who you're,
uh … What time is it?

Lincoln
It's three forty in the morning.

John Nicolay *(waking up)*
Don't … let him pardon any more deserters …

(Nicolay's asleep again.)

John Hay
Mr. Stanton thinks you pardon too many. He's generally apoplectic on the subject—

Lincoln
He oughtn't to have done that, crippled his horse, that was
cruel, but you don't just hang a sixteen year old boy for that—

John Hay
Ask the horse what he thinks.

Lincoln
—for cruelty. There'd be no sixteen year old boys left.

(*A beat, then:*)

Grant wants me to bring the secesh delegates to Washington.

John Hay
So ... There *are* secesh delegates?

Lincoln (scribbling a note, signing the petition)
He was afraid, that's all it was. I don't care to hang a boy
for being frightened, either. What good would it do him?

*(He signs the pardon. Then he gives Hay's leg a few hard
thwacks and a squeeze. It hurts a little. Hay winces.)*

Lincoln did pardon many soldiers accused of desertion and
other crimes. This was no fiction. He called them "leg cases."
Yet, he could be a hard man when necessary. Remember, this
is the commander in chief who allowed some 267 military ex-
ecutions. Although 303 Santee Sioux were sentenced to death
in the Minnesota uprising of 1862, this was the president who
authorized, after some hesitation, the hanging of 38 of the
insurgents—a mass execution. Thus, Lincoln was not afraid
to make hard decisions or impose hard policy. Clearly, it is
inconceivable that he would have simply stood by while ex-
Confederates wrested control of the postwar South away from
either the Congress or the president. Whether he would have
been successful in the long run is debatable. Certainly, his influence on events would have waned as he approached the end
of his second term in 1868. It is unclear what Lincoln would
have done if he had lived. What is clear is that the myth of
Lincoln's lost, tempered version of reconstruction has lived on
in popular memory.

3   "Let's Make a Start"

Women and Reconstruction

I'll sell my flax and my spinning wheel,
And buy my love a sword of steel,
Johnny has gone for a soldier.
I'll dye my dress, I'll dye it red,
And through the streets I'll beg for bread,
Johnny has gone for a soldier.
("Johnny Has Gone for a Soldier,"
Civil War song)

I was worn out from work and lonesome.
(Laurel's lament in *Sommersby*, 1993)

I need help, I need, I do need help.
(Ada's lament in *Cold Mountain*, 2003)

In 1861, Confederate women encouraged their men to join the fight against "Yankee aggression." But with Johnny Reb "gone for a soldier," women had to assume duties that would ordinarily fall to the men. In time, as the war dragged on year after year, their faith in cause and country eroded. At first women demonstrated a determination and patriotism that reflected their belief in the cause and in victory. Manning plantations and farming the land, however, proved a heavy burden. And, with the men gone, they feared their inability to control the slaves. By 1864, optimism gave way to defeatism—as reflected in anger against perceived government incompetence, food shortages, and the death of their menfolk.[1] At the end of the war, 25 percent of Southern white men of military age were dead. A war that had begun as a romantic dream had become a nightmare. The life of many elite white women, women of the yeomen class, and poor whites in the Civil War and Reconstruction were fraught with uncertainty, deprivation, threats of violence, and even death, especially during the chaotic years of 1864 and 1865 as defeat of the Confederacy came closer. At the end of the war, women had to redefine their lives and negotiate their place in a society and economy undergoing fundamental stress. They had, in essence, to reconstruct their lives in a reordered world. For those women who endured the war alone, the return of their men also involved readjustment. Women had learned to be independent in a society that prized paternalism. For many women the return of the husband involved difficult choices about their status in the relationship. Were they to welcome the return to dependency or fight to keep their independence? Two Hollywood films, *Sommersby* (1993) and *Cold Mountain* (2003), bring to the screen aspects of Reconstruction dealing with the relationship between women and men during a time in which the old relationships, family, race, and economics had to adjust to a new reality—a South transformed by war.

SOMMERSBY: HOMECOMING

In this film set during Reconstruction, the hero of the film attempts to create a new economy (raising tobacco rather than cotton) and a new racial order (poor whites and poor blacks uniting for a better future). Nothing like this happened during Reconstruction. Poor whites, both men and women, were as committed, perhaps more so, to white supremacy as former masters. Courageous and imaginative leadership might well have changed the South for the better. But no such leadership emerged. Indeed, the long white insurgency against Reconstruction was sustained because white people, elite and common, were invested in the old racial order. Slavery no longer existed but race control still mattered. Nevertheless, *Sommersby* is, in some ways, an imagining of W. E. B. Du Bois's Marxist-influenced Freedom Road history of Reconstruction and Fast's *Freedom Road.*

The movie had its origin not in an American novel about the war like *Cold Mountain,* discussed below, but rather as an Americanized remake of a 1982 French film: *The Return of Martin Guerre.* In the Middle Ages, a man returns after years away from his village in France and identifies himself as Martin Guerre. After a time, suspicions are aroused; the man is arrested, tried, and executed for the impersonation. In the movie Martin Guerre becomes Jack Sommersby, a Confederate veteran.

The original is set during the Hundred Years' War; the American remake is set in north-central Tennessee in the months immediately following Lee's surrender. The film introduces actor Richard Gere as Jack, who returns from the horrors of the war changed in every possible way. His racial attitudes are positively enlightened, something that will separate him from his bigoted neighbors. Historian Jon D. Bohland observes that the film gives him "politically correct views on race, class, and women and offers the possibility of an easier life." Thus, the film presents a postmodern re-visioning of the southern soldier. He convinces his "wife" Laurel (Jodie Foster) who "passionately" accepts him as her missing husband. She is a survivor and the return of her "husband" suggests that a new life is possible.[2]

Jack is so enlightened and so transformed that he can rise above all pre-war prejudices. He is able to unite the entire population of his small town

> to reorganize the community into a farm collective, one where all of the town's citizen's—black and white, male and female—band together to buy their own portion of his former plantation land ... Despite some initial reluctance— "This town is finished, Mr. Jack"—on the part of many whites to share the land with former slaves, the citizens of Vine Hill ultimately support Jack's plan as their only alternative during a period of poverty and starvation.[3]

But Jack has enemies, particularly Orrin (Bill Pullman), who wants Laurel for himself (just as the villain Teague wants Ada in *Cold Mountain*) and succeeds in revealing Jack as really an "admitted swindler and Confederate deserter" named Horace Townsend who assumed Jack's identity after his death at the end of the war. In addition to the problem of the collective enterprise even succeeding, Jack and his "loyal" former slave—Joseph—must now deal with suspicious townspeople and an attack by the Ku Klux Klan. Despite everything, Jack's collective enterprise succeeds and the town is saved "from the economic and social ruin facing the rest of the South."[4] Jack's love for family, the soil, and his fellow man saves Vine Hill and redeems him. His cooperative farm rejects the racist tenant farming system that emerged after the war: "The film is vision of a populist, utopian South where black and white Southerners came together to *reconstruct* the South and each gains their own deserved piece of the American Dream …"[5] Laurel, for her part, plays the dual role of patient southern wife loyal to her husband. She is alone and newly poor—the "Yankees got all the silver, the carpets and mostly anything else they could carry." The town has been devastated by the war: "… everybody that ain't dead is leaving." Overwhelmed by economic ruin and feeling alone in the ruined South, she is tempted to marry Orrin. As she says: "I was worn out from work and lonesome." She keeps hoping for her husband's return after the long years of war *and* becomes an economic visionary to match her "husband" when he does "return." She offers her family heirloom—"I did save Granny's brooch"—to raise money to support the collective enterprise. And she knows from the start that "Jack" is not her husband.

Jack: Now, Laurel, you really believe I'm not your husband?
Laurel: Yes, you are not.
Jack: But you let everybody believe that I am. Why is that?
Laurel: Because I wanted you to be him as much as they [the townspeople] did.

Even after he is exposed as an imposter, Laurel remains loyal to him, having fallen in love with the new "sensitive" (and apparently sexually enlightened) Jack. She keeps loving him and bears their illegitimate daughter, Rachel (just as Ada bears Inman's child in *Cold Mountain*). True to the Lost Cause myth, "she ends the film tending to Jack's picturesque gravesite, a vision of the archetypically loyal and brave Confederate widow suffering alone after the war."[6] Once again, the Lost Cause myth finds new life. As Bohland argues:

> *Sommersby* ultimately relies upon many of the same racial, cultural, and gender stereotypes present in earlier Lost Cause inspired celluloid representations of the Old South. Jack's transformation in the film is a typical Southern redemption story, as he emerges from the war a pious and changed man. In rejecting his violent and wild past, Jack comes back from the war as the embodiment of the Southern gentleman, the fantasy model of Old South white masculinity made famous by Ashley Wilkes in *Gone With the Wind* and Confederate heroes such as Robert E. Lee and Stonewall Jackson. He transforms himself into an idyllic family man and member of the Southern patrician class.[7]

COLD MOUNTAIN: HOMEFRONT

Cold Mountain (2003) was directed by Anthony Minghella and based on the 1997 novel with the same title by Charles Frazier. The film is one of the very few Hollywood productions to deal with the Plain People of the South and their increasingly precarious position during and after the war. *Cold Mountain* illustrates that white women in many parts of the South (in this case, western North Carolina) "were physically threatened and attacked." It reveals as well the "social, political, and economic divisions that abounded" in the region and "the deprivation and scarcity became the normal pattern of life." Finally, it demonstrates that "the mountain counties were a center for deserters and Unionist sympathizers."[8] *Cold Mountain,* while not a perfect film, is remarkably accurate in dealing with one aspect of the plight of both elite and lower-class women and their hard scrabble life as the war came to an end. At the beginning of *Cold Mountain* Ada, in a voiceover, says: "War changed us beyond all reckoning."

Cold Mountain features Jude Law, Nicole Kidman, Renée Zellweger, Eileen Atkins, Philip Seymour Hoffman, Natalie Portman, and Donald Sutherland. Filmed in Romania, it made a profit of over eighty million dollars. With parts of the novel and film loosely based on *The Odyssey, Cold Mountain* tells parallel stories of the impact of the war on a specific Southern soldier and two women in the mountains of North Carolina. The soldier, W.P. Inman, reluctantly goes off to war in 1861 despite having no vested interest in the Southern "cause." He is especially reluctant because he has just met an educated, well-bred woman—Ada Monroe—(a woman above his station in life) who has moved into the area from Charleston—"world of slaves, corsets, and cotton"—with her minister father, Rev. Monroe.

Barely surviving the nightmarish Battle of the Crater in July 1864 during the siege of Petersburg, Inman, crouched in a trench as the battle rages and the corpses pile up, stares at a photograph of Ada. Lovesick and tired of war, he decides to desert and walk home to North Carolina—and to Ada. (It is a scene that references Ben Cameron gazing at a photograph of Elsie Stoneman in *The Birth of a Nation*). Inman's journey back also mirrors scenes in *The Odyssey* as many commentators have pointed out. Here are two examples: Inman and other deserters are lured into a hovel by what appears to be a bevy of promiscuous women. Inman resists their sexual invitations but the other men succumb, turning, figuratively, into Circe-transformed pigs. The deserters pay for their recklessness when they are betrayed to the Home Guard for a reward. Later, Inman comes across a Nausicaa figure, a lovely young widow who lives alone with her baby. She asks him to lie in bed with her and put his arm around her for the night. But there is no sexual contact. In the morning, Inman kills two Union soldiers who threaten the woman. She kills a third soldier, despite her earlier rejection of violence. Meanwhile, after her father dies, Ada finds herself with a farm she cannot keep up. She discovers that refined manners and piano lessons, although fashionable in Charleston, are not much use in rural North Carolina. Fortunately, a young country woman her age (Ruby Thewes) appears to teach Ada how to survive on the land in the absence of men.

*Scene. Front Yard. Black Grove Farm. North Carolina.
Late Afternoon, 1864*

*Ada Monroe is writing in her father's campaign chair, a blanket
wrapped around her, a farm rake propped up next to her.*

Ruby (off screen)
That cow wants milking.

*Ada looks up from her writing with a start. She covers
her letter, guiltily, instinctively. In front of her, at the gate,
is a young rawboned, feral woman of indeterminate origins.
She is barefoot, and dressed in a hand-dyed shift of blue.
Her name is Ruby Thewes.*

Ruby
If that letter ain't urgent, the cow is—is what I'm saying.

Ada
I don't know you.

Ruby
Old Lady Swanger says you need some help. Here I am.

Ada is instantly defensive, intimidated.

Ada
I need help, I need, I do need help, but I need a laborer—
there's plowing and rough work and—I think there's been a
misunderstanding.

Ruby
What's the rake for?

Ada
The rake?

Ruby
Ain't for gardening, that's for sure. Number one—you got a horse I can plow all day. I'm a worker. Number two there's no man better than me cause there's no man around who ain't old or full of mischief. I know your plight.

Ada
My plight?

Ruby
Am I hard to hear cause you keep repeating everything. I'm not looking for money, never cared for it and now it ain't worth nothing. I expect to board and eat at the same table. I'm not a servant. Do you get my meaning?

Ada
You're not a servant.

Ruby
People'll have to empty their own night jars, that's my point.

Ada
Right.

Ruby
And I'm not planning to work while you watch neither.

Ada
Right.

Ruby
Is that a yes or a no?

Ada (looks at Ruby)
Yes.

Ruby
There's half the day yet. Let's make a start. My name's Ruby. I know your name.

The two women survive but it's a hardscrabble existence. In addition to trying to scrape up enough to live on, the women are under siege by a monster figure—a Home Guard thug named Teague—who wants both Ada and her property. His henchman is the murderous psychopath Bosie.

Inman, overcoming many obstacles just like Odysseus, finally makes it home, manages to spend one passionate night with Ada, and then dies from a wound following a gunfight during which he kills the evil Teague and Bosie. The film ends with Ruby, now the mother of two children, married to a local man ("Georgia," a fiddle player). Ada is seen with her daughter, obviously the product of her one night with Inman. To echo her opening voiceover of how the war changed everyone, Ada offers a final comment: "What we have lost will never be returned to us."

Ada, Ruby, Inman, and the Historians

Women in this film are seen undergoing several real crises. James Inscoe, of the University of Georgia, writes of

> Ada Monroe, a refined and overeducated Charleston woman stranded on her recently deceased father's farm on Cold Mountain. She is totally unprepared to fend for herself in this foreign environment and is too proud to seek help from her generally sympathetic highland neighbors. Her salvation comes in the form of a brash mountain native who does know how to live off this land.

It is, he states, "an unlikely partnership" across the "cultural disconnect" of "elite and common women. ... Even more powerful—and more historically based," he continues "are other incidents that convey the brutal toll taken on mountain women, who as mothers, wives, and widows are forced to protect their families, sometimes violently retaliating against their tormentors."[9]

The depiction of the plight of Southern women, especially these mountain women, during the war also receives historical validation by Gordon B. McKinney who observes that

> Historians of the Confederacy have turned their attention increasingly to the home front to find an explanation for the collapse of the southern army and government in 1865. Both works of broad synthesis and narrow specialization have concluded that the destruction of civilian morale was the crucial factor that led to the massive number of desertions that left the Confederate armies unable to resist Federal advances. Moreover, several scholars have argued that women played a central role in the decline of southern willingness to sacrifice for the cause.[10]

In his journey home, Inman meets a mountain woman (Maddy the Goat Woman) who saves his life, shelters him, and savages the "Lost Cause" mythology even as he admits that he was "Like every fool sent off to fight with a flag and a lie." Even more bluntly savaging the "Lost Cause," Maddy asks him, "What I want to know is, was it worth it, all that fighting for the big man's nigger?" At one point after he is captured by a rag-tag Home Guard troop, Inman says he will not go back to the army to be killed for a cause that he does not believe in. It is not just Inman who lacks attachment to the cause but, as the war progressed, the women as well. Consider film historian Jenny Barrett's evaluation of *Cold Mountain*. The film

> is very much concerned with the effects of war. In particular, it is remarkable in its treatment of women. Women are seen to survive torture, to run a farm as efficiently as a male workforce, to live in harmony with nature, to show generosity beyond measure and to kill to protect their own. Even Ada, whose personal Self Civil War might seem initially to be one of how to survive deprivation, can be found at the end of the film violently beating Teague with the butt of a rifle. Ada, Ruby, Sally, Sara and Maddy are each vivid

tributes to the women who fought to survive the Civil War, bereaved, starving, and lonely ... the critical viewer might even understand the film as one that *re-writes the master narrative of the Civil War—a narrative that in Hollywood has so far been almost exclusively written by men—in which the part of the woman is to sew a flag for her sweetheart and weep over his coffin.* It is Ruby, after all, who, on the news that Teague and his men have shot her deserting father, says "Every piece o' this is man's bullshit! They call this war a cloud over the land, but they made the weather and then they stand in the rain and say, shit! It's rainin."[11]

On the other hand, the film also maintains the myth in several crucial ways. James Inscoe (and others) remind us that "Neither slavery nor slaves play much of a role in the story."[12] At the actual Battle of the Crater, over six hundred black soldiers were slaughtered by Southern troops. In the battle scene, *one* black, Union soldier is seen fighting *one* Confederate soldier who is a Native American (since *Cold Mountain* was filmed in Romania for economic reasons, there were no African Americans available to portray the hundreds of black soldiers fighting for the Union on that day; soldiers from the Romanian Army were used). Barrett comments that there is

barely a single black face in the film ... a slave family is seen on the run, only to be slaughtered off-screen, and an establishing shot of a plantation house-cum-hospital shows black slaves picking cotton ... Slavery is not overtly discussed ... later a neighbor comment[s] that Ada has decided to free her father's slaves. An interview with the black director Spike Lee makes an interesting point about this absence: "We're going backward if *Gone With the Wind* is more progressive than *Cold Mountain*. *Gone With the Wind* was made in 1939. In 2004 we're not even in it? We're going backward. I don't understand it." What this comment indicates is that even the most contemporary of Civil War films continue to hail the white American ancestor but not his black counterpart, *Glory* and *Gods and Generals* aside. Considering that the resolution of *Cold Mountain* is the revelation of Ada having borne a child to Inman, and since the family of the Civil War domestic melodrama is representative of the nation, the film clearly *depicts the birth of a new, white nation,* the most apparent ideal of which is the capacity to overcome any hardship for the sake of love.[13]

The birth of a "new white nation" was also the climax of *The Birth of a Nation.* Movies and the culture they reflect have not progressed much as one might expect in the eighty-eight years that separate the two films.

Harsher criticism of the film comes from Robert M. Myers, who finds that "The most consistent and intriguing differences between the novel and the film are in their representations of the ideology of the Lost Cause."[14] Myers traces the origin of the expression "Lost Cause" to the title of Edward A. Pollard's history of the Confederacy. Over the decades the phrase mutated in a variety of ways but never relinquished its essential meaning and the coming of film only reinforced it. The first three premises of the Lost Cause voiceover (others were added later) were enunciated in the 1870s by the Southern Historical Society:

First, they insisted that the South fought for states' rights, not slavery. Second, they represented Robert E. Lee as a military genius and a perfect embodiment of the Southern gentleman. Finally, they claimed that, despite the heroism of the individual Confederate soldier, the North's overwhelming resources and numbers eventually forced the South to succumb ... [Also] much of the nationalization of Lost Cause ideology can be attributed to two immensely popular epic films ... *The Birth of a Nation* ... and ... *Gone With the Wind* ... While not as popular as these earlier works, *Cold Mountain* in its novel and film versions perpetuate the mythology of the Lost Cause.[15]

Inman's cynicism about the war reflects a rejection of a central element of the Lost Cause:

> Old Lee ... said it's a good thing war is so terrible or else we'd get to liking it too much. As with everything Marse Robert said, the men repeated that flight of wit over and over, passing it along from man to man, as if God almighty Himself had spoken. When the report reached Inman's end of the wall he just shook his head. Even back then, early in the war, his opinion differed considerably from Lee's, for it appeared to him that we like fighting plenty, and the more terrible it is the better. And he suspected that Lee liked it most of all and would, if given his preference, general them right through the gates of death itself.[16]

As he deserts and travels through the flatlands of North Carolina on the way to his beloved mountains, Inman thinks to himself, "How did he ever think this to be his country and worth fighting for?" When he passes through a region with large mansions, he bitterly realizes "he had been fighting for such men as lived in them, and it made him sick."

In the novel, the women reinforce Inman's apostasy. When he takes shelter with Maddy (called "the goat woman") in the novel and protests against her comment about "fighting for the big man's nigger," the goat woman

> insists that slavery is the real cause of the war: "Nigger-owning makes the rich man proud and ugly and it makes the poor man mean. It's a curse laid on the land. We've lit a fire and now it's burning us down. God is going to liberate niggers, and fighting to prevent it is against God."

Later, when the young widow

> Sara tells him that her husband was killed at Gettysburg, he completes the process of effacing any meaningful cause for the war: "Every man that died in that war on either side might

just as soon have put a pistol against the soft of his palate and blown out the back of his head for all the meaning it had."

Myers sees Frazier, in the novel, constantly "undermining" the tenants of the Lost Cause, for example, in the myth's "emphasis on the Northern superiority of numbers." In the novel, Inman had turned away in disgust at the slaughter of Union troops at the Battle of Fredericksburg (as he would later at the Battle of the Crater).

When he is with the goat woman, Inman regrets his initial enthusiasm for the war. "The shame he felt now to think of his zeal in sixty-one to go off and fight the downtrodden mill workers of the Federal army, men so ignorant it took many lessons to convince them to load their cartridges ball foremost."

And the women are just as skeptical. Ada responds to a "long and maudlin story" by a neighbor about Southern troops facing "dreadful odds" with the dismissive comment that the story is "the most preposterous thing I have ever heard." In contrast, Myers notes, Minghella ignores much of Frazier's critique of the Lost Cause.[17]

Myers argues:

Minghella's *Cold Mountain* reflects the Lost Cause interpretation most pointedly on the origins of the war. In contrast to Lost Cause ideology, the film identifies slavery as the fundamental cause, but Minghella carefully distances the main characters from the issue ... Minghella represents the economic interests of the wealthy planters as the real cause of the war, a cause hidden from most of the men who will fight.

In the film, Inman tells Ada's father that the South is fighting to keep things as they are.

Thus ... he enlists to protect the South he loves, whereas in the novel, he comes to a more complex realization that it was boredom that seduced him into military service. In any case, both screenplay and film *take pains to demonstrate that he does not enlist to defend slavery; indeed many of Minghella's changes to the novel distance Inman from the racism of the region.*[18]

Race plays a minor role in the film so that "the only racists in the South seem to be the members of the despicable Home Guard." Myers adds that a scene cut from the final version "echoes the message of *The Birth of a Nation* when [Teague] promises to 'guard against the Negro. They want what the white man got. Give them the chance, they'll carry rape and murder to your firesides.'"[19]

Ada's final voiceover in Cold Mountain laments that "what we have lost will never be returned to us" and "The land will not heal. Too much blood. The heart will not heal. All we can do is make peace with the past and try to learn from it." But, as Myers tells us, "the lesson from the past is to avoid war, but the *film's final image draws on Lost Cause affirmations of Southern perseverance, reinforced by images of music, family, and religion.*"[20]

At war's end women faced new challenges—to economic and social status and to domestic relationships. Some would assume new roles and many would return to a patriarchal dependency characteristic of life before the war. For their part the men tried to reassert their privileged position in a society. But in many cases, men were no longer able to support their families let alone continue to be slave masters. Some elite women assumed new independent roles, but many others became the keepers of the flame of Confederate memory—erecting monuments and nursing the memory of rebel manhood.[21] Thus *Cold Mountain* and *Sommersby* are to be praised for including the plight of Southern women during the war and after it into the standard narrative. On the other hand, they must also be charged, yet again, even into the twenty-first century, with perpetuating the misleading assertions of the Lost Cause.

4 "Sunshine Headin' My Way"

Memories of Reconstruction in Black and White

Zip-a-dee-doo-dah, zip-a-dee-ay
My, oh my, what a wonderful day
Plenty of sunshine headin' my way
Zip-a-dee-doo-dah, zip-a-dee-ay
Mister Bluebird's on my shoulder
It's the truth; it's actual
Ev'rything is satisfactual
Zip-a-dee-doo-dah, zip-a-dee-ay
Wonderful feeling, wonderful day, yes
Sir!

("Zip-a-dee-doo-dah"
from *Song of the South*)

WALT DISNEY'S RECONSTRUCTION

At the end of October 2011, The Walt Disney Company released a new video game: *Kinect Disneyland Adventures*. The video game features three animated characters from Disney's film *Song of the South* (1946)—in the game, players join Brer Rabbit, Brer Fox, and Brer Bear in the "The Briar Patch," "The Log Flume," and "The Barrel Run" down a virtual Splash Mountain.

The movie brought to the screen Southern writer Joel Chandler Harris's *Uncle Remus: His Songs and His Sayings* (1880), a series of thirty-nine fables based on African folklore. Now, the company's promotional copy for the game invites us to "delve into the murky waters with Brer the [*sic*] Rabbit."

Set on a Reconstruction-era Georgian plantation, *Song of the South* was a technically innovative film for its time, combining live action and animated scenes. The Uncle Remus stories of Brer Rabbit, Brer Fox, and Brer Bear, as told by the kindly black "uncle," come alive as cartoon inserts in the story of a young white boy learning to deal with the separation of his parents.

The year 2011 also marked the sixty-fifth anniversary of the release of the film that won two Academy Awards. Black actor James Baskett, who played Uncle Remus, received a non-competitive honorary Oscar "for his able and heartwarming characterization of Uncle Remus, friend and storyteller to the children of the world"; "Zip-A-Dee-Doo-Dah" won the Oscar for Best Original Song. The song, in fact, became the theme for the popular *Wonderful World of Disney* television series, 1969–1979. The longevity of both the Uncle Remus stories and its dubious progeny—*Song of the South*—is quite remarkable. Recognizing the potential for controversy because of its patronizing portrayal of African Americans, however, Disney has refused to authorize re-release of the movie. It is now available only in unauthorized editions. It has become a cult film, reflected in an unauthorized website—www.songofthesouth.net—devoted to the movie.

Yet, unwilling to give up the commercial potential of the cartoon characters, the company, before the marketing of the video games, had created a theme-park ride, Splash Mountain, at Disney locations in Anaheim, California, Orlando, Florida, and Tokyo, based on the Brier Patch.

Historian Jason Sperb views the actual Splash Mountain theme-park ride and the film *Song of the South* in the context of American cultural and racial history. He notes that, although most audiences (members of the National Association for the Advance of Colored People excepted) thought the film innocuous, "Uncle Remus is a controversial figure who suggests that blacks lived in extreme poverty, but were nonetheless happy and content alongside their former owners, still faithfully serving the rich whites and their children during the Reconstruction era in the American South." He goes further in stating that "with Splash Mountain, Disney effectively pulled the original roots of *Song of the South* out from under the film." Now, "Splash Mountain represents a commodified , homogenized version" of "a now distant ... relative"—Uncle Remus.[1]

This is not what Joel Chandler Harris intended. He drew his stories from African folktales as told by black people on the cotton and rice plantations of the South. They were intended to convey the wisdom of the downtrodden in their own authentic dialect. As he explained:

> The story of the Rabbit and the Fox, as told by the Southern negroes, is artistically dramatic in this: it progresses in an orderly way from a beginning to a well-defined conclusion, and is full of striking episodes that suggest the culmination. It seems to me to be to a certain extent allegorical, albeit such an interpretation may be unreasonable. At least it is a fable thoroughly characteristic of the negro; and it needs no scientific investigation to show why he selects as his hero the weakest and most harmless of all animals, and brings him out victorious in contests with the bear, the wolf, and the fox. It is not virtue that triumphs, but helplessness; it is not malice, but mischievousness.[2]

The use of the stories, nevertheless, was more complicated within the context of Southern race relations. As Jennifer Rittenhouse points out, when the stories first appeared in 1879 and 1880, "white southern readers scarcely waited for the ink to dry before they began offering personal testimonies to the authenticity of the ... representations of black character and plantation life."[3] Whereas for generations black southerners had been using the Brer Rabbit tales at the heart of Harris's narratives to teach their own children lessons about the survival in a decidedly brutal and unjust world, white southerners read them differently. What they took away from the stories was the loyal uncle's "love for his white folks, especially the white child" and by implication an idyllic world lost to a destructive Civil War and to the oppression and disruption of the Reconstruction years.[4]

In 1946, however, it was perfectly acceptable to continue to present on film that plank of the Lost Cause platform that emphasized the contented lives of black people in the postwar South and the affectionate relationship between white and black Southerners—an extension of the antebellum master–servant relationship and their mutual sense of community.

The original stories were placed in the Edenic Old South world so dear to the Lost Cause industry; the film, however, is set *after* the war. The blacks are no longer slaves but they are just as content as if they still were. They sing a great deal. They sing on the way back from the fields; they sing just walking along by themselves as Uncle Remus does; they sing while baking pies; they sing in sympathy, fearful that Johnny, the child hero of the story, is dying after being trampled by a bull. *Song of the South* brings into the twentieth century via film one of the most influential series of stories and characters in late nineteenth- and early twentieth-century American literary, cultural, and even political history. The world of African Americans, both before *and* after the Civil War (as long as they remained faithful and well behaved), was one long "wonderful day" with "plenty of sunshine headin'" their way. The truth, as the Lost Cause myth would have it, was that every day "Ev'rything is satisfactual" so "yes sir!" how could there not be a perpetual "wonderful feeling, wonderful day."

THE FANTASY WORLD OF SOUTHERN RACE RELATIONS

In the 1880s and 1890s, writers such as George Washington Cable, Thomas Nelson Page, and Joel Chandler Harris created a literature that historian David Blight observes "delivered an almost retrievable world of idyllic race relations and agrarian virtue." The stories are peopled with thoroughly stock characters:

> Southern gentlemen ... gracious ladies ... and the stars, the numerous Negro mammies and the unwaveringly loyal bondsmen. In virtually every story, loyal slaves reminisce about how the era of slavery—"befo' de war"—before freedom left them lonely, bewildered, or ruined souls in a decaying landscape. Their function in the new order is to tell stories of the old days; they are the sacred remembrancers of the grace and harmony of the Old South.

By a stroke of what can only be called perverse genius, many of these stories are narrated by the slaves or ex-slaves themselves in what came to be accepted as authentic Negro dialect. The result: "A civil war among whites—the torn fabric of the nation—is mended by the wit, wisdom, and sacred memories of faithful blacks" and "How better to forget a war about slavery than to have faithful slaves play the mediators of a white folks' reunion."[5]

More influential, more popular, more long-lasting were Harris's Uncle Remus stories. Harris was a man of contradictions whose stories enriched the Lost Cause myths yet who, as an editor of *The Atlanta Constitution,* attacked Southern racism and supported education, voting rights, and equality for blacks. (In 1926, Harris's son Julian LaRose Harris and Julian's wife, Julia Collier Harris, won a Pulitzer Prize for their fight against the Ku Klux Klan.)

Harris's Uncle Remus first appeared in 1877 as an old black man with tales about Atlanta. Harris's collection *Uncle Remus: His Songs and Sayings,* published to national and international acclaim, became a perennial bestseller by 1880. Indeed, the appeal of these stories was so great that the wily Brer Rabbit became one of the most popular literary figures of nineteenth-century American literature.[6] White Southerners read the stories through the lens of white supremacy and, like Disney a century later, they removed the stories from their original African-American context.

Uncle Remus memorably delivers a message that 1890s, Americans—North and South—wanted to hear. "They needed increasingly," Blight argues, "to believe that their terrible war had little to do with race. But at the same time, they needed melodious black voices telling them tales of a little creature's heroism against the forces of power and privilege. Uncle Remus delivered both messages." The enduring appeal of the Uncle Remus stories, through the first half of the twentieth century, certainly must have been one of the reasons Disney chose to create a mitigated version of the stories in 1946.[7] A title card at the beginning reveals the approach to history that the film will take: "Out of the humble cabin, out of the singing heart of the Old South have come the tales of Uncle Remus, rich in simple truths, forever fresh and new."

The Civil War is over; in fact it is not even mentioned. The blacks are not slaves but appear as "employees" on the plantation of Miss Doshy whose daughter Sally is married to John, an Atlanta newspaper man. They travel to the plantation with their son Johnny and his black nursemaid Tempy. John insists that he must return to Atlanta, which causes friction between the unhappy couple and propels Johnny to run away. Fortunately, he runs into the kindly Uncle Remus who had told Sally and John stories when *they* were children. His first story tells Johnny the near unpleasant fate of Brer Rabbit when he tried to run away from home.

At various points in the film, Uncle Remus tells Johnny other stories of Brer Rabbit, the trickster Brer Fox, the eternally frustrated pursuer of Brer Rabbit, and Brer Bear, the dim-witted accomplice of Brer Fox. These tales are animated and focus on Brer Rabbit's cunning in escaping the clutches of Brer Fox and Brer Bear who intend to make a meal of him.

Johnny befriends a black boy, Toby, and a "poor" white girl, Ginny Favers, both his age. In contrast, he has trouble with Ginny's bullying brothers, Jake and Joe. The brothers are mean to everyone, including their sister whose puppy they threaten to drown. Ginny gives the puppy to Johnny but his mother refuses to let him have it so he prevails upon Uncle Remus to care for it.

Johnny learns to use reverse psychology on the brothers from another Brer Rabbit story and both brothers end up being spanked by their mother. This intensifies their antagonism to Johnny and, in revenge, they ruin the pretty dress that their mother makes for Ginny when she is invited to Johnny's birthday party.

Eventually, Johnny's mother demands that Uncle Remus stop telling him stories and to stay away from the boy. A sad Uncle Remus plans to leave the plantation and go to Atlanta. When Johnny hears the news he charges across an open field to stop Uncle Remus but is trampled by an angry bull. Seemingly on his death bed, Johnny is revived by the arrival of his father and by the return of Uncle Remus who starts to tell the story of Brer Rabbit and his "laughing place."

Johnny has a miraculous recovery and, at the end of the film, as he, Ginny, Toby, and the puppy skip down a lane, they and Uncle Remus are suddenly joined by the animated characters from the stories and they all skip along singing "Zip-A-Dee-Doo-Dah."

ROLE OF A LIFETIME

The depiction of blacks in American film from the very beginning in the late 1890s and even, in many cases, to the present moment (George Lucas, for example, has asserted that he had trouble getting funding for his World War II epic *Red Tails* because it had an all-black cast), calls to mind the title of Ralph Ellison's great novel about the black experience in America, *Invisible Man.* With *Song of the South,* not much had changed since 1915 (*The Birth of a Nation*) or 1939 (*Gone with the Wind*); in fact Hattie McDaniel had only gone from Mammy in 1939 to Tempy, the nurse maid, in 1946. Even when blacks appear on-screen, in whatever minor roles are assigned to them, they are essentially invisible. Uncle Remus, the beloved story-teller, has no existence other than telling his stories. He has no inner or even outer life. His past, present, and future are of no interest. This is the story and the fate of black characters in *Song of the*

South. If they are not passive, supportive companions to their masters, their life has no other purpose. Further, Hollywood's Reconstruction makes no mention of the cost of black liberation and the price that Uncle Remus paid for his freedom. He is happy merely to serve as a teller of tales and a companion of children.

DYING FOR FREEDOM: THE COST OF LIBERATION

The Civil Rights movement and the end of Jim Crow at least provided for a more complex and comprehensive depiction of African Americans in film and in Reconstruction historiography. *Glory* (1989), coming forty-six years after *Song of the South,* attempts to challenge some of the Lost Cause myths by emphasizing black self-emancipation. The movie depicts the forming and subsequent fate of the 54th Massachusetts Volunteer Infantry, the first formal unit in the US Army to be made up entirely of African-American men under the leadership of their white commanding officer Robert Gould Shaw. The film was a moderate financial success but it received Academy Award nominations for Best Editing and Best Art Direction, as well as a number of British Academy Awards and Golden Globe Awards. Denzel Washington received an Academy Award for Best Supporting Actor. For the first time in a "major motion picture" Hollywood told a Civil War story from a black perspective, albeit with a white man in the lead role.

In the film, Captain Robert Gould Shaw (Matthew Broderick) is wounded at the Battle of Antietam (1862) where his regiment suffers heavy losses. As he recovers from his wounds, he learns that Abraham Lincoln is about to issue the Emancipation Proclamation. Shaw is promoted to Colonel and given command of the first all-black regiment. His first volunteer is a Boston friend, an educated black man named Thomas Searles (Andre Braugher). As the unit forms, many black men volunteer including an escaped slave named Trip (Denzel Washington), a free black named Jupiter Shart (Jihimi Kennedy), and a gravedigger named John Rawlins (Morgan Freeman). The men train hard but are assigned to menial tasks. When Shaw realizes what is happening, he confronts his two commanding officers General Charles Garrison Harker (Bob Gunton) and Colonel James Montgomery (Cliff De Young), both of whom are involved in war profiteering. Gould threatens to report them both to the War Department if the 54th isn't sent into combat.

Initially, the unit faces derision and ridicule from white Union troops but they prove themselves in a minor battle in South Carolina where they defeat a Confederate attack. Unfortunately for Shaw and for most of the 54th, he volunteers the unit to lead the attack on Fort Wagner in Charleston, South Carolina. Along with two brigades of white troops, the 54th attack Fort Wagner on July 18, 1863.

The film's epilogue reveals that Fort Wagner was never captured by Union troops. But it also states that news of the courage of the 54th spurred black recruitment into Union armies and that by the end of the war more than 180,000 African Americans were serving.

As a historical aside, it should be noted that Shaw and most of his men were buried in a mass grave which the Confederates considered an insult. After the battle, the bodies of other Union officers were returned. Confederate commander General Johnson Hagood, however, refused to return Shaw's corpse, declaring "had he been in command of white troops, I should have given him an honorable burial: as it is, I shall bury him in the common trench with the negroes that fell with him." Shaw's father publically announced that he was *proud* to know that his son was buried with his troops. He wrote to the regimental surgeon: "We would not have his body removed from where it lies surrounded by his brave and devoted soldiers ... nor wish him better company,—what a body-guard he has."[8] So, in death, ironically Shaw became one with all the "invisible men" he had led into battle. What was intended as an insult became a tribute.

Even more importantly, the role of blacks in the Civil War—almost completely ignored in the triumph of Lost Cause memory in the 1880s and 1890s—was affirmed and re-affirmed in the monument to Shaw and the 54th that was unveiled in Boston on Memorial Day, May 31, 1897. Blight discusses the significance of the memorial. Nearly 3,500 individuals marched to the front of the State House, including 140 survivors of the black 54th and 55th Infantry and the 5th Cavalry. The stone monument depicts Shaw astride his horse:

> Behind, and as though surrounding Shaw, march his black volunteers, ladened with knapsacks and canteens. With muskets darting upward at angles, their bodies arched forward, the soldiers flow inexorably toward their fate. The faces of the troops (twenty-three in all on the relief) capture the individuality, their shaven youth and bearded middle age, their dignity and resolve ... As the monument sweeps the eye forward, it foreshadows a tale of how commander and men will die together.[9]

The year before the unveiling, the Supreme Court in *Plessey v. Ferguson* "enshrined the 'separate but equal' doctrine (announced with virtually no press coverage or public outcry)." Even more telling, between 1897, when the Memorial was unveiled, and 1906, whites lynched at least 884 blacks. Only three days after the unveiling, mobs broke into a jail in Urbana, Ohio where many of the 54th volunteers had come from, and lynched a man named Charles Mitchell, accused of assaulting a white woman.[10] The "Invisible Men" were about to become even more *invisible* for the next six decades.

The pride in self-emancipation and joy of freedom came at a cost. Historian Leslie A. Schwalm describes the tribulations of black people during the Civil War and Reconstruction, noting that wartime emancipation had "two intertwined developments." First, the conditions of slavery worsened on the plantations and farms of the Confederacy as the economy declined. Second, those who grabbed their freedom through self-emancipation by leaving their owners and fleeing to the Union lines often faced horrible conditions, frequently made worse by the prejudice of Union officers. As many as 400,000 to 500,000 out of approximately four million slaves escaped to the Union-occupied areas during the war. But there was a high price to be paid.

Malnutrition, disease, and violence were not uncommon for those remaining within rebel territory. But "contrabands," as those who fled were called, faced tough conditions as well—overcrowded contraband camps were riddled with disease—"diarrhea, dysentery, cholera, typhoid, measles, mumps, smallpox, yellow fever, and tuberculosis."[11] Black women and children fared the worst.

Historian Jim Downes also tells the hard story of black liberation in *Sick from Freedom* (2012). He surveys, for example, the wave of sickness that swept through the free black population between 1862 and 1870 that took some 60,000 lives. He emphasizes as well how both traditional and revisionist accounts of Reconstruction ignored this history. In other words, African Americans paid a high price for freedom on the battlefield and on the sickbed from abuse and neglect. He calls disease "the unexpected enemy." Thus, "when historians narrate the transition for slavery to freedom, they often emphasize the thrill of freedom ... which has the unintended effect of diminishing the grueling process that was actually emancipation." This is the neglected side of liberation and Reconstruction—a story of people "dying to be free." Yet, "The destruction of slavery," he argues, "left little rhetorical room for freed people to articulate how emancipation was a glorious achievement but one that brought new struggles that threatened their survival."[12]

Despite the suffering, no one wanted to return to captivity. If nothing else, this alone puts the lie to any nostalgic view of the plantation communities, slavery as a benign institution, and the *Song of the South*. Yet the South won Reconstruction as evidenced by the triumph of the Redeemer governments by 1877 and the onset of the dismal years of segregation and white supremacy in the 1890s. What the South lost in the war it regained at the end of Reconstruction.

For freedmen and freedwomen there was a victory as well. The hardships of liberation were accompanied by a vision of freedom's potential to create a new bi-racial world. Remarkably, the ex-slaves did not demand revenge or retribution. What black people wanted was an economic and political system open to all—black as well as white. They wanted a nineteenth-century version of the promise of America. The achievements of the so-called carpetbag governments in the South in which black men participated as legislators may have been short-lived but these achievements were remarkable for the time—public schools systems, state constitutional reform, expansion of voting rights, and adoption of the Thirteenth, Fourteenth, and Fifteenth Amendments. The immediate achievements were eventually undermined by the paramilitary insurgency, the return of conservative Democrats to the polls, and the abandonment of the freedmen by the North. Nevertheless, African Americans have seen Reconstruction years not as a dystopian world, as conservative whites did, but as a time of celebration and struggle in face of determined opposition. It took over a century for the story of black military service, black self-emancipation, and the cost of black liberation to become part of the Civil War and Reconstruction narrative.

5   Wilkes & Kennedy, Inc.

War and the Destruction of the Old Order

> There was a land of Cavaliers and Cotton Fields called the Old South … Here in this pretty world Gallantry took its last bow. Here was the last ever to be seen of Knights and their Ladies Fair, of Master and of Slave … Look for it only in books, for it is no more than a dream remembered. A Civilization gone with the wind …
>
> (Opening title of *Gone with the Wind*, 1939)

The destruction caused by Sherman's March through Scarlett's Georgia in 1864 during the Civil War transformed the "pretty world" of the antebellum South. The economic destruction (although often exaggerated) and the wartime neglect of the economy in the South offered possibilities furnished by "creative destruction"; that is, the destruction of the old economic system could have given way to the opportunities for a new economic order. But without adequate access to credit, poor black farmers (including black independent farmers) as well as their former owners had little prospect for economic progress. The system of tenant farming and share cropping that replaced the old plantation system only ensured enduring poverty.

The failure of the will or the imagination to see opportunity for a meaningful transformation of the South after the war had multiple consequences. A progressive approach to rebuilding the South was possible, but never tried. Heather Cox Richardson argues that a kind of Marshall Plan (when US aid helped to rebuild Europe after World War II) for the South. After all, the Federal government had used its resources to encourage private development of the transcontinental railroads. Such thinking was not beyond the realm of possibility.

The combination of race, the reactionary culture in the South, and the reluctance of the North to invest in the Southern economy prevented a Marshall-like solution. Then, to compound the problems of the postwar South, in the first part of the twentieth century, alien invaders again crossed the land to wreck new havoc on the land of the Cavaliers—the boll weevils.[1]

Eventually Scarlett's Atlanta did recover but not until the Second World War. Cotton continued to be the cash crop of the region. The Georgia Piedmont region sank into a deep and persistent poverty. And the social and political culture remained resistant to "Yankee" progress and change.

While Reconstruction in *The Birth of a Nation* is seen as a political and racial evil that must be destroyed, in *Gone with the Wind* it is a series of obstacles, chiefly economic, set against the story of two strong-willed lovers—Rhett and Scarlett. With its emphasis on the combative love relationship between Rhett and Scarlett, *Gone with the Wind* is not as obsessed with reasserting white supremacy as Griffith was; here the postwar struggle is essentially economic, not racial, as reflected in Scarlett's obsession with money and saving Tara, the family plantation. The Civil War transformed the Southern economy. Destruction wrought by the Union armies and the ambiguous labor relationships brought about by emancipation required an imaginative approach to solving postwar economic problems. Reconstruction was seen primarily as a political and racial struggle and the opportunity to reform the South economically through imaginative government action was lost. Students need to consider the economy of the postwar South as an essential part of the Reconstruction story and the issue of lost opportunities in history.

Scene: Atlanta, Georgia, 1865
Scarlett: Have you a store? This?

Frank: Won't you come in, look around a bit? (Into the store) I don't suppose it looks like much to a lady, but I can't help being proud of it.

Scarlett: You're not making money?

Frank: Well, I can't complain. In fact I'm mighty encouraged. Folks tell me I'm just a born merchant. It won't be long now before Miss Suellen and I can marry.

Scarlett: Well, you're doing as well as all that?

Frank: Yes, I am, Miss Scarlett. I'm no millionaire yet, but I have cleared a thousand dollars already.

Scarlett: And lumber too?

Frank: Well, that's only a sideline.

Scarlett: A sideline, Frank? With all the good Georgia pine around Atlanta, and all this building going on?

SCARLETT'S RECONSTRUCTION

The seemingly innocuous exchange, quoted above, between Scarlett O'Hara and Frank Kennedy is actually fraught with meaning for Scarlett, and for the past, the present, and the future of the South. Scarlett has come to Atlanta to see Rhett Butler in the hope that he will give her the money to pay the taxes on Tara, otherwise the O'Haras will lose the house and land forever. Unfortunately for Scarlett, Butler is in jail—temporarily as it turns out—and has no access to the fortune he acquired as a blockade runner during the war. Scarlett wanders into the general store of Frank Kennedy, a plain middle-aged man who is engaged to marry her sister Suellen. As the exchange above indicates, Frank is having some success in postwar Atlanta as a merchant. Seizing the opportunity, Scarlett tells Frank that Suellen is interested in another man, and within two weeks she marries Frank and, of course, is given the money to pay the taxes on Tara.

Not content with being the wife of a merchant, Scarlett—to the disproval of Atlanta—becomes one herself and an incredibly successful one. She runs Frank's business and gets rich; she buys a saw mill—for that Georgia pine—and shrewdly offers Ashley

Wilkes the position of manager, thus insuring he stays close to her. She has a child, Ella Lorena, her second, with Frank (her first, Wade Hampton, was from her very brief marriage to Melanie's brother when the war begins in 1861). In the film, neither child exists; Scarlett's first and only child (with Rhett Butler) is Eugenia Victoria—Bonnie Blue—who dies at four in 1873. Frank, who in the novel is a member of the Ku Klux Klan, is killed by Union troops during the raid on the shantytown where Scarlett was attacked by two men, one white, one black, but saved by Big Sam, a former slave from Tara. The film excludes any mention of the Klan; instead Frank is just one of a group of irate citizens who attack the shantytown in retaliation for the attack on his wife.

Jenny Barrett suggests that Scarlett assuming the role of business woman has multiple implications:

> If the film is approached as having a two-part structure (Civil War and Reconstruction periods), a whole sequence of oppositions can be discovered between themes, values and characters across the two segments, i.e. the war/post-war; loss of the old South/building of the new South and so on … the Rhett/Ashley opposition … create[s] a list of related dichotomies … that … correspond to the two-part structure: new South/old South, commerce/plantation, realism/idealism.

These dichotomies can be seen to be represented "by Melanie and Ashley (old) and Scarlett and Rhett (new). The 'old' values and qualities are those of generosity, honor, and monogamy and those which are 'new', as displayed by Scarlett and Rhett are selfishness, dishonor, and polygamy." Melanie, for example, only marries once; Scarlett has three husbands. Barrett concludes:

> The dichotomies are symbolized … by many elements in the text. Rhett's sentiment about the upholders of the Southern lost cause is that they are "living in the past," contrasting with Scarlett's final declaration that "tomorrow is another

day." The commerce and plantation opposition is symbolized by the two products, timber and cotton. One is integral to the literal re-building of the South and its exploits the Union, the other is the lynchpin of the old Southern economy and exploits the slaves ...[2]

Since Scarlett's transitions from Southern belle (the old South) to successful businesswoman (the new South), it is important to review the intensity of the change. Barbara Welter describes the kind of "education" and "training" young women in the nineteenth century were exposed to both North and South so that they could become and remain "true women." Welter writes:

Woman, in the cult of True Womanhood presented by the women's magazines, gift annuals, and religious literature of the nineteenth century, was the hostage in the home ... The attributes of True Womanhood, by which a woman judged herself and was judged by her husband, her neighbors and society could be divided into four cardinal virtues—piety, purity, submissiveness, and domesticity. Put them all together and they spelled mother, daughter, sister, wife— woman, without them, no matter whether there was fame, achievement or wealth, all was ashes. With them she was promised happiness and power.[3]

Is there a better description of Melanie Wilkes or of half of Scarlett's personality as the war begins? The war changes everything in general and specifically for Scarlett. It gives her the opportunity to break free from true womanhood. Scarlett comes to repudiate the "submissiveness" aspect of the cardinal virtues. And she had a huge obstacle to overcome. Welter comments:

Submission was perhaps the most feminine virtue expected of women. Men were supposed to be religious, although they rarely had time for it, and supposed to be pure, although it came awfully hard to them, but men were the movers, the doers, the actors. Women were the passive, submissive

responders. The order of dialogue was, of course, fixed in
Heaven. Man was "woman's" superior by God's appointment, if not in intellectual endowment, at least by official
degree ... Women were warned that if they tampered with
this quality they tampered with the order of the Universe.[4]

No wonder Scarlett, the "new" postwar Scarlett, provokes
such anger. Before and during the war, she is just a Southern
belle who has gone astray from Mitchell's description of her
early in the novel. Elizabeth Fox-Genovese provides the description that takes Welter's observations right into the heart of *Gone
with the Wind:*

> She knew how to smile so that her dimples leaped, how to
> walk pigeon-toed so her wide skirts swayed entrancingly,
> how to look up into a man's face and then drop her eyes
> and bat the lids rapidly so that she seemed a-tremble with
> gentle emotion. Most of all she learned *to conceal from men
> a sharp intelligence beneath a face as sweet and bland as a
> baby's* ... at sixteen she looked sweet, charming and giddy,
> but she was, *in reality, self-willed, vain and obstinate.*[5]

It doesn't seem likely that Mitchell knew the following statement. Too bad because its sheer inanity suggests why the "new"
woman, North and South, was destined to emerge. Welter
quotes Dr. Charles Meigs from "Lecture on Some of the Distinc-
tive Characteristics of the Female" delivered at Jefferson Medical
College, Philadelphia in January, 1847: "Woman has a head
almost too small for intellect but just big enough for love."[6]

Both Welter's and Fox-Genovese's essays are treasure houses
of examples of absurdities about the inferiority—physical, intellectual, emotional—of women and why they must be forever
dependent and childlike. Scarlett, by a combination of choice
and necessity, pushes back against nearly all these rules by the
combination of the obstinacy of her nature and the tribulations
imposed on her and her family by the war. It would be a mistake
to conclude that *Gone with the Wind* represents a proto-feminist

polemic. As will be discussed below, Mitchell may have chosen "to wed Scarlett to the death and rebirth of the South,"[7] but she also wed herself to the myths of the Lost Cause as the novel, as opposed to the film, makes endlessly clear.

Scarlett's emergence as a "mover, doer, actor" in Reconstruction Atlanta stands in sharp contrast to the pallid behavior of the males in her life. He first husband—Charles Hamilton—dies of pneumonia and the measles two months after marrying Scarlett and enlisting in the rebel army. Her second husband—Kennedy—easily manipulated into marriage suddenly finds that the belle of Tara has cast off true womanhood:

> Frank was not only amazed at his wife's views and her plans but at the change which had come over her in a few months since their marriage. This wasn't the soft, sweet, feminine person he had taken to wife. In the brief period of the courtship, he thought he had never known a woman more attractively feminine in her reactions to life, ignorant, timid and helpless. Now her reactions *were all masculine.* Despite her pink cheeks and dimples and pretty smile, *she talked and acted like a man* ... She knew what she wanted and she went after it by the shortest route, *like a man,* not by the hidden and circuitous routes *peculiar to women.*[8]

Scarlett, for her part, sees Frank as one whose time has come and gone: "Frank might have been a successful business man in the easy days before the war but he was so annoyingly old-fashioned ... and so stubborn about wanting to do things *in the old ways, when the old ways and the old days were gone.*"[9]

Frank's survival skills are no better than Charles's. When he and Ashley and others raid the shantytown where Scarlett was attacked and avoided rape only through the intervention of Big Sam, formerly a slave at Tara, only Frank ends up, at Rhett puts it bluntly to Scarlett: "dead. Shot through the head."[10]

Of course, even more than Frank there is the plight of the hapless Ashley Wilkes, Scarlett's "true" love. The war transforms the perfect cavalier into a shadow of his former self. He comes back a broken man. He has every intention of leaving the South for a job in the North before Scarlett convinces him to manage her saw mill. No matter how he contracts as Scarlett expands, she still idolizes him as the perfect man and always throws him in the face of Rhett as his polar opposite. Finally Rhett can stand it no longer and forces Scarlett to face the truth about her cavalier, after she accuses him of hating Ashley. The exchange in the novel reads:

Rhett: I don't hate him any more than I like him. In fact, my only emotion toward *him* and *his kind* is pity.
Scarlett: Pity?
Rhett: Yes, and a little contempt. Now, swell up like a gobbler and tell me that he is worth a thousand blackguards like me and that I shouldn't dare be so presumptuous as to feel either pity or contempt for him. And when you have finished swelling, I'll tell you what I mean if you're interested.
Scarlett: Well, I'm not.
Rhett: I shall tell you, just the same, for I can't bear for you to go on nursing your pleasant delusion of my jealousy. I pity him because he ought to be dead and he isn't. And I have contempt for him because he doesn't know what to do with himself now that his world is gone.
Scarlett: If you had your way all the decent men in the South would be dead.
Rhett: And if they had their way, I think Ashley's kind would prefer to be dead. Dead with neat stones above them, saying: "Here lies a soldier of the Confederacy, dead for the Southland" or "Dulce et decorum est"— or any of the other popular epitaphs.[11]

Rhett goes on for several pages forcing Scarlett, against her will, to see Ashley whole.

Scarlett protests the Ashley is unhappy because he lost all his money. Rhett replies: "I tell you it's losing their world—the world they were raised in. They were raised to be certain persons, to do certain things, to occupy certain niches. And those persons and things and niches disappeared forever when General Lee arrived at Appomattox ... What is Ashley Wilkes to do, now that his home is gone and his plantation taken up for taxes and fine gentlemen are going twenty for a penny. Can he work with his head or his hands? I'll bet you've lost money hand over fist since he took over the mill."[12]

FROM GRIFFITH TO SELZNICK

The Birth of a Nation had an incredibly negative impact on race relations in the United States but, by 1939, "talking pictures," as they were first called, were over a decade old and silent films had retreated to the margins of public attention. The year 1939 was a golden year for motion pictures. Unfortunately, among the most golden was a film that—in a less savage fashion—continued the damage done by Griffith twenty-four years earlier.

Consider our "counterfactual" film review from *The New York Times* in 1939:

David O. Selznick's *Gone with the Wind*, perhaps the most eagerly awaited and eagerly anticipated film in the history of the movies opened last night in Atlanta to what turned out to be a less-than-thunderous reception from its predominantly Southern audience. Mr. Selznick has taken Margaret Mitchell's enormous bestseller, originally published in 1936, and turned it into a combination romantic spectacle in full color *and* a somber meditation on the sad consequences of the use and misuse of history, particularly the history of what we know as the "Reconstruction" period after the Civil War. In what can only be a deliberate repudiation of D. W. Griffith's *The Birth of a Nation,* which came to the screen almost twenty-five years ago, Mr. Selznick has created the longest sound film made to date—three hours and forty-four minutes (Griffith's film in 1915 was the longest film ever made at that date)—and has achieved pioneering effects with the new magic of color cinematography (Griffith's film was memorable, from a technical point of view, for several cinematic innovations). The central love story of Mitchell's novel is retained and the performances of Clark Gable, Vivien Leigh, Olivia de Havilland, Leslie Howard and a cast of dozens are all enthralling to behold. But Mr. Selznick's main interest seems to lie in "correcting" the terrible distortions of Reconstruction history that made Griffith's film so destructive despite its many cinematic achievements. In an interview prior to the film's premiere, Mr. Selznick spoke at length about his determination to use his film to enlighten audiences—both those who actually may have seen and remember *The Birth of a Nation* and the millions who have read and re-read *Gone with the Wind*. In both cases, the realities of the post-Civil War South have led to a mistaken set of impressions and conclusions about slavery, about the causes of the war, about the plight of the freed slaves, and about the positive aspects of Reconstruction. Mr. Selznick admitted that what he has undertaken is a daunting task and that his fidelity to fact rather than to the myths of the "Lost Cause" may turn *Gone with the Wind* into a box office bust rather than the bonanza his studio still hopes for. In addition to perpetuation of the myths in Griffith's film and Mitchell's novel, Mr. Selznick had to confront, as he calls it, the "pseudo-history" of the so-called Dunning School of Reconstruction history, a series of books by William Dunning of Columbia University and his many acolytes in academia who, for decades, have passed off as accurate an astonishing collection of half-truths and outright lies about the period. Mr. Selznick concluded that he hopes that even if *Gone with the Wind* doesn't find a mass audience of viewers at least he will be remembered as a filmmaker who tried to use the power of film to make a positive and constructive comment on the history of race in America.

Of course, no such review appeared. The real *Gone with the Wind* would define the Old South and Reconstruction into the twenty-first century.

One thing positive that can be said about the film version of Mitchell's novel is that it omits most of the more virulent racism. That may be the one positive statement that can be made about the film. *Gone with the Wind* has had a long and deeper impact on cultural consciousness than *The Birth of a Nation*. Today, only film buffs—especially silent films buffs—film, social, and cultural historians, and film history classes have any interest in *The Birth of a Nation* despite the fact that a DVD version was released in 1998 and 2011 saw the release of a "special" three-disc DVD version *and,* the ultimate compliment, a Blu-ray version. On the other hand, is there a man, woman or child in America who has not seen *Gone with the Wind* either on VHS or DVD (including a Blu-ray edition on its seventieth anniversary—November 14, 2009) or on network television, or on cable television, or even during an occasional theatrical re-release, e.g., in 1947, 1954, 1961, 1971, 1974, 1989, and 1998. Griffith's film was made before the movies began to ply themselves with awards. *Gone with the* Wind was nominated for thirteen academy awards and achieved eight wins (including Best Picture) plus one honorary and one technical Oscar (the most for any film until *Ben Hur* (in 1959) and, until 1966, was the highest grossing film of all time until overtaken by *The Sound of Music.* Is there a man, woman, or child in this country who hasn't turned to someone and said, "Frankly my dear, I don't give a damn"?

Mitchell was born in 1900 and no doubt saw *The Birth of a Nation* at some point in 1915 or 1916. She began to write the novel in 1926 while recovering from an auto accident, coincidently during the six-year period (1924–1930) when the deification of Robert E. Lee had another upsurge. Published in 1936, *Gone with the Wind* is the only novel Mitchell published in her lifetime. Actually, she had no need to even try to write another novel; *Gone with the Wind* has sold far in excess of thirty million copies since its publication. The 1999 paperback reprint calls it "America's Most Beloved Epic Novel" and "The Greatest Love Story of All Time ..." Like Griffith's film, *Gone with the Wind,* novel and film, has essentially a two-part structure: part one—just before and during the Civil War—and part two—the aftermath of the war including Reconstruction.

An intertitle early in *The Birth of a Nation* which describes the planter class and plantation culture of the antebellum South as "where life runs in a quaintly way that is to be no more" is just as appropriate to the opening scenes of *Gone with the Wind*. At Tara, the home of the O'Haras, and at Twelve Oaks, neighboring large cotton plantations, all is young love, flirtations, and "moonlight and magnolias." The war suddenly intrudes interrupting the attempts of willful, headstrong Scarlett O'Hara to win the love of that epitome of Southern genteel manhood Ashley Wilkes. Into this Edenic landscape wonder two intruders—one public, one private—in the form of the Union Army and the charismatic womanizer Rhett Butler. Both will play a major role in the lives of Scarlett, her family, her friends in particular and the South in general. To cope with the eventual defeat, the "plantation myth" comes into being. The "plantation myth," as outlined by Bruce Chadwick and found fully developed and assumed by both Griffith and Mitchell, postulates that

> the old South was a special place ruined forever by history's lightening: 1) all white Southerners were rich plantation owners and, in their personal lives, well-educated, romantic cavaliers; 2) white Southerners loved their slaves and their slaves loved them and they all just wanted to be left alone; 3) the North started the war, forcing the gentlemen of the South to fight the Lost Cause for four long years, to lose in the end, but lose gallantly; 4) the South was devastated by Reconstruction—imposed by the federal government—and never recovered. *Gone with the Wind*, seen by just about every American in theaters and, later, on television, had the power to reinforce these myths and turn them into acceptable fact.[13]

With its emphasis on the combative love relationship between Rhett and Scarlett, *Gone with the Wind*, is not as obsessed with reasserting white supremacy as Griffith was. Between her own mercenary abilities and Rhett Butler's millions, Scarlett is able not only to completely rebuild Tara but to also build and inhabit the finest mansion in a re-built Atlanta in the years after the war.

And yet, and yet, *Gone with the Wind* makes palpable and more easily digestible the crude racial assumptions and other fantasies of the "Lost Cause" mythology. In the long run, it is a much more dangerous film.

THE ECONOMIC CONSEQUENCES OF THE WAR

At the conclusion of his history of the Lost Cause, Pollard surveyed the "spectacle of ruin, the greatest of modern times":

> There were eleven great States lying prostrate; their capital all absorbed; their fields desolate; their towns and cities ruined; their public works torn to pieces by armies; their system of labor overturned; the fruits of the toil of generations all swept into a chaos of destruction; their slave property taken away by a stroke of the pen; a pecuniary loss of two thousand millions of dollars involved in one single measure of spoliation—a penalty embraced in one edict, in magnitude such as had seldom been exacted unless in wars synonymous with robberies.[14]

Scarlett's business interests reflect the need for rebuilding in the post-Civil War South. Her ambition and ruthlessness is reflected not only in her relations with men but also in her engagement in the convict lease system whereby prisoners were leased by the state to labor for contractors such as Miss Scarlett. Most of the military campaigns conducted in the South resulted in the destruction of the railroad system, towns, plantations, public buildings, factories, bridges, and farms. The war also saw the neglect of the levees that protected the Mississippi delta region and the dislocation of Southern foreign and domestic commerce. Further, emancipation ruined the investment in slaves and made worthless the Confederate currency. The extent of the destruction and the nature of the war have occupied the attention of historians. Was the Civil War an example of total war or at least a precursor to the level of economic and civil mobilization and the massive material and human destruction of the truly indisputably total wars of 1914–1918 and 1939–1945?

Consider the most famous (or infamous) example of economic warfare in the Civil War—the burning of Atlanta and Sherman's March across Scarlett's Georgia and then into the Carolinas (November to December 1864)—events replicated in both *The Birth of a Nation* and, most famously, in *Gone with the Wind.* How bad was it in the South at the end of the war?

One study, based on the observations of a Captain John Rziha, the chief of topographical engineer of the XIV Corps of Sherman's army who kept a detailed account of the movement of the Yankee passage through the Georgia Piedmont region along a sixty-mile stretch from Covington to Milledgeville, observed the long-term consequences of the March. From this account, historian D. J. de Laubenfels concludes that the region was changed fundamentally by the event but also explodes some of the myths of the Old South. "What the soldiers saw," he states, "was a civilization taken by surprise, its ordinary affairs disrupted." It was a modestly prosperous land—the antebellum mansions were located primarily in the towns. The local inhabitants referred to a cluster of buildings on a farm as a "plantation." And the so-called plantation headquarters were no more than a single house or cabin.[15]

Sherman's soldiers conducted a thorough invasion across central Georgia. They carried off all the food they could lay their hands on. Temporarily this meant hunger or even starvation in Georgia but food included also seed and livestock, the basics of future production. Slaves, the human-labor factor, were set free—many to wander about aimlessly for a time.

The system of tenant farming and share cropping that replaced the old plantation system only ensured enduring poverty.[16] Perhaps it did not have to be this way, as Richardson tells us. Was a counterfactual history possible? Was the South really predestined to endure a century and more of poverty?

Whatever the realities of the story, the physical destruction of the South was alloyed to the myth of the Lost Cause. Here, for example, the people of Columbia, South Carolina lament their defeat and the wreck of their homeland in *The Passion of Jonathan Wade,* an opera by Carlisle Floyd, first produced in 1962 and then revised in 1990. It is the story of Reconstruction in Columbia from April to November 1865. According to the libretto,

> *the curtain rises on the faintly lit outline of a devastated city. It is daybreak and vaguely discernible in the spectral quiet are rows of fire-scarred chimneys, standing like silent sentinels over the remains of houses and buildings. People in various attitudes of quiet and patient waiting as the lights gradually come up. There is an atmosphere of total dejection and spiritual desolation as the people wait, each isolated within himself:*

> **People of Columbia sing** (the chorus):
> It is done: the war is over
> And we who are left endure.
> Fields are scorched where corn once grew;
> The earth is sour and its crops is weeds.
> Broken bricks, blackened by fire,
> Litter gardens where flowers bloomed.
> Our cities and homes, once ordered and proud,
> Are now embalmed in rubble heaps,
> And we are left to endure.[17]

Thus, the Reconstruction South remains ever the victim in the popular mind—left to endure in a perfect state of preservation like fossil set in amber.

6 "I Am Vengeful and I Shall Not Sleep"

The Civil War and the Legacy of Violence during Reconstruction

> The region was an American underbelly in the semi-tropical heat; the manners were softer, the violence swifter, the commerce slower, the thinking narrower, the past closer.
>
> (George Parker, "Southern Discomfort,"
> *The New Yorker*, January 21, 2013)

In 1866, Southerner Edward A. Pollard (1831–1872), a former journalist with the *Richmond Examiner*, reflected on the meaning and limits of defeat:

> The war has not swallowed up everything. There are great interests which stand out of the pale of the contest, which it is for the South still to cultivate and maintain. She must submit fairly and truthfully to *what the war has properly decided*. But the war properly decided only what was put in issue: the restoration of the Union and the excision of slavery; and to these two conditions the South submits. But the war did not decide negro equality; it did not decide negro suffrage; it did not decide State Rights, although it might have exploded their abuse; it did not decide the orthodoxy of the Democratic party; it did not decide the right of a people to show dignity in misfortune, and to maintain self-respect in the face of adversity. And these things which the war did not decide, the Southern people will still cling to, still claim, and still assert in them their rights and views.[1]

Pollard admitted, if reluctantly, that secessionist theory was dead and slavery as an institution had been "excised." He was firm, however, about the determination of white Southerners to hold to their core cultural, political, and racial values—Southern pride, Southern honor, and Southern white supremacy.[2] This resistance to the full consequences of military defeat and the reluctance of most white Southerners to engage in the protocol of defeat (admitting they were wrong on the issues and acknowledging defeat) motivated the anti-Republican, anti-Reconstruction insurgency.

In the traditional interpretation of the resistance to the consequences of defeat and to Reconstruction the image of violence took on a patina of romance; the Ku Klux Klan appeared as knights of the Southland who used violence only reluctantly and in defense of white civilization. In the climactic scene in *The Birth of a Nation* for example, Klansmen, summoned by hilltop buglers, ride to the rescue of Southern women besieged by black soldiers. The true story of Reconstruction violence, however, was far different and far from romantic. The Klan was a manifestation of a general insurgency aimed at the restoration of Southern racial customs and control following emancipation as well as the overthrow of Republican state governments. Violence was endemic in the South—a feature of Southern frontier culture. Yet, after the Civil War, as Geroge Rable puts it, "the extraordinary violence of the Reconstruction period … erupted because white southerners in 1865 found their world turned upside down."[3] But anti-Reconstruction violence was also a legacy of the violence of Civil War itself—a continuation of what the unreconstructed viewed as the continuing struggle against Yankee reformism.

VIOLENCE GLORIFIED: *THE BIRTH OF A NATION*

In *The Birth of a Nation,* terror is an honorable strategy for reordering Southern society. The freedmen, the film asserts, must know their place in a white civilization.

Ben Cameron returns to South Carolina at the end of the war, surviving both his wounds and the attempt to hang him as a guerilla. Thanks to the pleas of his mother and Elsie Stoneman and, of course, the pardon issued by "the Great Heart," Ben can now attempt to return to the life he knew before the war. But that, of course, is impossible; those "quaint" days are gone forever. Reconstruction is underway and not under the compassionate leadership of Abraham Lincoln—"our best friend is gone"—but rather under the whip of the venomous Radical Republicans as embodied in Austin Stoneman and his white, and worse, black allies. In a conversation, the mulatto—Silas Lynch—bows to Austin Stoneman who tells him "you are equal to all here" and sends Lynch south to Piedmont to preside over Reconstruction there. "The blight of reconstruction," as the intertitle proclaims, quoting Woodrow Wilson, has the goal of putting "the white South under the heel of the black South." Lynch immediately begins to encourage the Piedmont blacks to quit working for their former white masters. On the personal side, one glimpse of Elsie Stoneman before he leaves for South Carolina inflames his desire for a "white" wife.

The Freedman's Bureau is established and denounced as a "charity of the North to delude the ignorant" (the blacks of course). Everywhere whites are insulted; a black soldier pushes Dr. Cameron around. Griffith makes it clear that there are now the "good" Negroes still loyal to the Old ways and the new "bad" Negroes who want power. The Cameron's loyal "Mammy" disdains Stoneman's free black "servant": "dem free niggers from the North sure are crazy." Lynch, who can't keep his eyes off of Elsie every time they meet, condescends to Ben Cameron who is so outraged by his behavior that he refuses to shake hands with Lynch.

Things go from bad to worse for white Southerners. The "franchise" is extended to blacks "who don't know the meaning of the word." On election day, nearly every black votes while whites are turned away from the polling places. The carpetbaggers and the blacks win; Lynch is elected Governor. Ben Cameron's anger grows as he compiles a list of outrages against whites. His old servant is whipped for "not" voting and a black elder is shot for trying to help him. All these outrages culminate in the infamous

"Historical Facsimile" (actually based on satirical anti-black cartoons rather than photographs as the film claims), *Riot in the Master's Hall.* The "Negro" Party is now in control of the South Carolina House of Representatives—101 blacks overwhelming 23 whites in the year 1871. The blacks conduct themselves as drunken clowns, one taking his shoes off, one putting his feet up on his desk, and many others eating and guzzling liquor. They pass a law requiring white civilians to salute black officers and now comes the real horror: allowing mixed-race marriage. Thus Thomas Dixon's sexual nightmare comes to pass in Griffith's film.

THE SEXUALIZED COMPONENT OF VIOLENCE

Michael Rogin in his study of *The Birth of a Nation* connects Dixon's sexual Negropobia to Griffith's:

> The liberty blacks wanted, Dixon and Griffith insisted, was sexual. "Equality, Equal Rights, Equal Politics, Equal Marriage" reads a placard in the black-dominated South Carolina legislature [no such placard is known to have ever existed]. Griffith and Dixon accused *Birth*'s opponents of promoting miscegenation. Dixon called the NAACP the Negro Intermarriage Society and claimed it "hates *The Birth of a Nation* for one reason only—it opposes marriage of blacks to whites." One purpose of *Birth,* Griffith boasted, "was to create a feeling of abhorrence in white people, especially white women, against colored men." Griffith and Dixon imagined a monstrous America of the future, peopled by mulattoes. Stopping black men from penetrating white women gave birth to a redeemed nation … Mixture of blood from "the surviving polygamous and lawless instincts of the white male" Dixon wrote … had "no social significance': the offspring of black mothers were black. But give Negro men access to white woman and they will destroy "the foundation of racial life and civilization. The South must guard with flaming sword every avenue of approach to this holy of holies." And beyond

Dixon and Griffith, both before and after, there is more, always and ever more: "The southern woman with her helpless little children in a solitary farm house no longer sleeps secure," warned the president of the University of North Carolina in 1901. "The black brute is lurking in the dark, a monstrous beast, crazed with lust. His ferocity is almost demonical."[4]

THE INVENTION OF THE KLAN

Suddenly Ben Cameron has an epiphany. He observes some white children, wearing white sheets, pretending to be ghosts to scare black children. Since all blacks are essentially children, Ben conceives the idea of the Ku Klux Klan—adult men wearing sheets to scare and control the out-of-control blacks. The Klan is formed and a "lustful" black named Gus, a freedman and soldier, gives them the opportunity to begin a campaign of terror. Flora Cameron goes off alone to fetch water. Gus accosts her and tells her that he wants to get married. Terrified, Flora flees deeper into the woods, pursued by Gus. Trapped at the end of a convenient precipice, Flora leaps to her death when Gus refuses to back away. Ben, who had been searching for his sister, finds her and holds her as she is dying. Taking a Confederate flag and dipping it in Flora's blood, Ben and the Klansmen find Gus, try him, find him guilty, and leave his corpse on the doorstep of Silas Lynch.

Governor Lynch shows Gus's body to Stoneman and orders the black militia to crack down on the Klansmen. Meanwhile, Elsie Stoneman breaks her engagement to Ben Cameron after her father tells her, "Your lover belongs to a gang of murderers." On their side, the Klansmen decide that all blacks have to be disarmed.

THE KLAN AS HEROES

Dr. Cameron is arrested for having Ben's Klan costume, a crime punishable by death. Margaret Cameron comes to Elsie asking help to save her father. Phil Stoneman, Margaret's lover, kills a black soldier to defend Dr. Cameron who, along with Margaret, takes shelter in a small hut occupied by two former Union soldiers who agree to hide them. An intertitle declares, "The former enemies of North and South are united again in defense of their Aryan birthright." Unaware that her father is not home, Elsie goes to Lynch asking for compassion for the Camerons. He proposes marriage and Elsie threatens him with a horse-whipping. Even more inflamed, Lynch tells Elsie she will be the "queen of his black empire."

As all these parallel events take place, the Klansmen are summoned to action! Now is the time for the full weight of terror to fall on the presumptuous and newly arrogant blacks.

Lynch orders a quick, forced marriage and hides Elsie as Stoneman returns. He tells Stoneman that he wants to marry a white woman and Stoneman approves ... until ... Lynch reveals that it is Elsie, which angers Stoneman. Klansmen discover Elsie's plight and goes for help. Now the might of the Klan exerts itself. Ben and the Klansmen race to rescue Elsie and arrest Lynch. As the Klan celebrates the rescue, news comes of the danger to Dr. Cameron and Margaret. Ben and the Klan ride out and arrive just in time to save those in the cabin and to disarm Lynch's militia.

This is glorification of terror, not the inglorious terror of both *Ride with the Devil* and *Cold Mountain*. These terrorists are not the unwashed, toothless, sadistic psychopaths and near-psychopaths of the Bushwackers or the Home Guard who ruthlessly kill men, women, and children. These Klansmen, led by Ben, are the cavalier noblemen restored to their rightful place as both the guardians of the social order and the protectors of the sexuality of white women (the "Holy of Holies" according to Dixon). The Klan celebrates its victory with a grand march through Piedmont, terrifying the blacks and relieving the white people of their fears of a Black Empire (and, of course, of intermarriage).

The spectacle of the liberation of Piedmont gives way to a conclusion perhaps even more shocking as the deity is invoked to bless the triumph of white over black. As Ben and Elsie and Phil and Margaret enjoy a joint honeymoon, the final moment of the film shows the god of war fading as the image of Christ takes its place. The final intertitle proclaims: "Liberty and Union, One and Inseparable, Now and Forever."

So terror is validated and Griffith's history of Reconstruction succeeded on a larger scale; the film helped in the ongoing revival of the Ku Klux Klan that began in 1913 and really took off in 1915 (the year *Birth* was released).

The intensity of feeling in whites provoked by *The Birth of a Nation* can be seen as a direct result of the ways in which the film validates the fantasies of the "Lost Cause" by visualizing these fantasies in powerful and memorable scenes. The overriding goal of what can be called "The Lost Cause Corporation" is the unrelenting desire to control the public memory of the war and *Birth,* along with decades of corporate output, was a key element in perpetrating the myth of Northern oppression and justifying the violent insurgency led by the unreconstructed. George Rable concludes: "former Confederates had achieved through political terrorism what they had been unable to win with their armies—the freedom to order their own society and particularly race relations as they saw fit."[5] Tragically, for almost a hundred years after Reconstruction the Southern insurgency was portrayed as necessary, even honorable.

SEEDS OF DESTRUCTION

The origins of anti-Reconstruction violence lay in the vicious, irregular war in the Border States during the Civil War. This Confederate resistance became a model for the Ku Klux Klan and other anti-Reconstruction paramilitary groups.

Ride with the Devil (1999), a film that focuses on the bloody guerrilla raids by rebel William Quantrill during the war, illustrates this legacy of violence. The movie follows the fates of four young men, including a freed slave who remains "loyal" to the former master who freed him. They end up as Southern guerrillas—"Bushwackers"—and join up with Quantrill for the raid on Lawrence in 1863. They are Southerners but they have no particular allegiance to the Southern cause; they have drifted into the Bushwackers for personal rather than political reasons. The movie illustrates how the hard realities of the border war set the precedent for the anti-Reconstruction insurgency.

Eighty-four years earlier *The Birth of a Nation* justified the same terroristic violence that *Ride with the Devil* (and *Cold Mountain*) exposes and condemns. The white South must be kept from being put "under the heel of the black South." Ben Cameron—the little Colonel pardoned by "the Great Heart"—invents the Ku Klux Klan as the instrument to terrorize the newly freed and animalistic, raping blacks into submission to white dominance. His own sister had leaped to her death rather than submit to the lust of a freed slave.

It can be argued that the South won the Reconstruction by a combination of counter- Reconstruction violence and the "non-violent" control of the historical narrative of Reconstruction. In other words, what was lost in the Civil War was regained in part in the insurgency that infected the Reconstruction years. The experience of war carried over to the Reconstruction period. Violence was married to a particular historical narrative—to usable history.

Scene: Kansas, August 1863

Mr. Evans
You ever been to Lawrence young man?

Jack Bull Chiles (scoffs)
No, I reckon not Mr. Evans. I don't believe I'd be too welcome in Lawrence.

Mr. Evans
I didn't think so. Before this war began,
my business took me there often. As I saw those
northerners build that town, I witnessed the seeds
of our destruction being sown.

Jack Bull Chiles
The foundin' of that town was truly the beginnin'
of the Yankee invasion.

Mr. Evans
I'm not speakin' of numbers, nor even abolitionist trouble
makin'. It was the schoolhouse. Before they built their church,
even, they built that schoolhouse. And they let in every tailor's
son … and every farmer's daughter in that country.

Jack Bull Chiles
Spellin' won't help you hold a plow any firmer.
Or a gun either.

Mr. Evans
No, it won't Mr. Chiles. But my point is merely that they
rounded every pup up into that schoolhouse because they
fancied that everyone should think and talk the same
free-thinkin' way they do with no regard to station, custom,
propriety. And that is why they will win. Because they believe
everyone should live and think just like them. And we shall
lose because we don't care one way or another how they live.
We just worry about ourselves.

Jack Bull Chiles
Are you sayin', sir, that we fight for nothin'?

Mr. Evans
Far from it, Mr. Chiles. You fight for everything that we ever
had, as did my son. It's just that … we don't have it anymore.

(*Ride with the Devil*, 1999)

TERROR AS STRATEGY AND POLICY

At the conclusion of Daniel E. Sutherland's study *A Savage
Conflict: The Decisive Role of Guerrillas in the American Civil
War* (2009), he explains the origins of the violent resistance to

Reconstruction by the ex-rebels. The South, he writes, would not "soon escape the legacy of violence, vigilantism, and outlawry spawned by the guerilla warfare." The anti-Reconstruction violence of the Ku Klux Klan, the Knight of the White Camellia, and other paramilitary gangs used "the rifle, the knife, and the rope" to kill and intimidate their Reconstruction opponents. The tactics of guerilla warfare were applied now to contest the war's political and racial settlement.[6] What white Southerners could not win on the battlefields of 1861–1865, they would win by other means.

Director Ang Lee's 1999 film *Ride with the Devil* (based on the novel *Woe to Live On* by Daniel Woodrell) takes up the question, directly and indirectly, of terrorism as an insurgent strategy and a political policy during the Civil War. Specifically, the film's key scene recreates the attack on Lawrence, Kansas, on August 21, 1863 by approximately four hundred Southern Bushwackers.

In *Ride with the Devil,* Lee presents terroristic activity on both sides but his focus is chiefly on the Bushwackers and especially Quantrill and other Confederate partisans. His emphasis is on the Southern-led campaign of violence in Kansas and Missouri during the war.

Lee tells the story of four Southerners brought together by a variety of circumstances that push them into joining the Bushwackers. Jake Roedel is the son of German immigrants who identify with his Southern friend Jack Bull Chiles and rejects the pro-Union sympathies of his father and the larger German community in Missouri. The murder of Chiles's father by Kansas pro-Union "Jayhawkers" propels both men into the First Kansas Irregulars (the Bushwackers).

Later, they befriend two other men: George Clyde and former slave Daniel Holt whose freedom Clyde has granted and who thus remains loyal to Clyde even though he is now part of the pro-slavery guerila force. Jake had been warned by his father that Southern prejudice and fear of foreigners will always make him suspicious to the other Bushwackers—in fact he ends up being called "Dutchie" by the members of the gang. During an interlude when the four men take shelter with a Southern family—the Evanes—they meet a young widow—Sue Lee Shelley—who becomes romantically involved with Jack Chiles. Sue Lee is surprised at the presence of Daniel Holt who she calls a "nigger" and asks Clyde, "What is he doing here?" Clyde's reply shows a more tolerant sensibility: "He's not my nigger. He's just a nigger I trust with my life every day." The conversation quoted at the beginning of this chapter takes place during this "peaceful" interlude with the Evans family.

REVENGE

Meanwhile, Quantrill regroups his forces and plans a major raid on Lawrence that will bring together a force of 450 guerillas. Historically, the raid, according to Quantrill, was to take revenge for a Union attack on Osceola, Missouri in September, 1861, led by Senator James H. Lane, who lived in Lawrence. Osceola was sacked and nine men were executed. Quantrill declared that his motivation was "To plunder, and destroy the town in retaliation for Osceola."[7]

It is interesting that both *Ride with the Devil* and *Cold Mountain* feature, as a figure of unrelenting evil, a psychopathic killer whose allegiance to the South is merely a cover for wallowing in murder and sadistic violence. In *Cold Mountain,* it is the Home Guard companion of Teague, the monstrous "Bosie." In *Ride with the Devil,* it is the Bushwacker "Pitt Mackeson." This character becomes Jake's nemesis and enemy from the moment that Jake joins Quantrill's forces. He nicknames Jake "Dutchie" and is dubious about his loyalty to the South. In one episode Mackeson kills a storekeeper who had provided supplies to Union soldiers and, after killing the man, burns down the store, leaving the man's widow destitute. During the raid on Lawrence, Jake and Holt stop to have breakfast at a town restaurant. Mackeson enters and begins to verbally attack both men. Jake draws his pistol on Mackeson for a moment and makes it clear that Mackeson is more enemy than comrade-in-arms.

The raid on Lawrence is the centerpiece of *Ride with the Devil* and takes advantage of the abilities of filmmakers, since the Code collapsed in the late 1960s, to depict violence in the most graphic and explicit fashion. And this is true of every violent scene in the film. Jack Chiles suffers an arm wound that eventually leads to a bloody, screaming amputation that is physically and emotionally harrowing, one far different and more intense than the amputation scene in *Gone with the Wind*.

Barrett points out that one of the interesting aspects of *Ride with the Devil* is that, unlike *Gone with the Wind* and so many other "Lost Cause" productions, the film does not long for some Edenic past. There are none of the antebellum clichés about plantations and cavalier gentlemen in Civil War Kansas. Southern characters are seen in a sympathetic light but not the Southern myths.

> A farmer who offers supplies and a hiding place to Jake and his three companions, Mr. Evans tells them about the town of Lawrence [see dialogue above]. Evans sadly explains that the Northerners constructed a schoolhouse before anything else. Education for all meant that anyone could learn to think freely "with no regard to station, custom, propriety," and so, he implies, will live and think like Northerners. The tragedy of this, to Evans, is that the Confederacy would therefore lose the war because the South did not care about freedom and equality [the schoolhouse is seen in flames later in the film during the Lawrence raid]. He concludes by saying that the Bushwackers are fighting for everything the South has ever had but, in fact, they do not have it anymore. The sentiment is the opposite to that found in *Gone with the Wind* which longs for former days that were better for the plantocracy, not dreading days to come that are—ideologically speaking—better for all.[8]

The conclusion of the film looks to this idea that the future not the past should be the goal of the survivors. Jake and Holt, both wounded in a battle with Union soldiers, take shelter at the same residence where Sue Lee Shelley now lives with her baby girl, Jack's daughter.

> Although he is not the father and he considers marriage to be a *"peculiar institution" worse than slavery,* Jake develops a gruff affection for mother and child, and grudgingly marries Sue Lee. Jake's Self Civil War does not concern the temptation to fight … It is more concerned with a resistance to marriage and adult responsibility, despite an irresistible attraction to mother and child. On his first night as a married man, Sue Lee asks Jake if he is a virgin; he replies that he has killed fifteen men. He has clearly understood masculinity and maturity in terms of killing as opposed to sexual awareness.[9]

Jake, Sue Lee, and the baby leave Kansas for California, accompanied by Holt who plans to ride to Texas in the hope of finding his mother who was sold and sent there years earlier. In both cases, these two survivors are leaving the war before it ends (just like Inman in *Cold Mountain*) to seek a new life with a new configuration of family. On the way, they have one last confrontation with Pitt Mackeson but Ang Lee refuses to turn it into a bloody shoot-out such as the one that kills Inman at the end of *Cold Mountain*. Mackeson, obviously more insane than ever, declares he is returning to his home town where he wants to have a drink. This is seen as a suicide mission since the town is in Union hands and Mackeson will be shot on sight because of his savagery as a Quantrill raider. Barrett concludes:

> The closeness that develops between Holt and Jake confirms their shared philosophy, which is more characteristic of perceptions of the North, believing in the freedom and equality of all. The two men, black and white, form a new brotherhood of the American family, so far ideologically from the new white family at the end of *The Birth of a Nation. Ride with the Devil* affirms, then, the positive values of freedom and equality on a political level, and home and family on a personal level.[10]

THE LARGER MEANING OF *RIDE WITH THE DEVIL*

In contrast to Griffith's film with its valorization of terror, especially the kind directed against blacks, consider a contemporary
issue that Barrett raises at the end of her comments on the film. She
describes Mackeson as representing "something bad in the American psyche ... an element of the American character that craves
war and conflict." She quotes Daniel Woodrell, author of *Woe to
Live On,* a Vietnam veteran (and author of several savagely *noir*
novels set in drug-ravaged rural Missouri, one of which, *Winter's
Bone,* was made into a bleak and brilliant film in 2010):

> Woodrell felt distinct parallels between the motivations of
> young men in the 1860s and the 1960s. "There was a war and
> I just thought I should go," he says, but "got a crash course
> in what was really going on." Woodrell saw his novel being
> "as much about Vietnam and Bosnia as about Missouri and
> Kansas." Certainly, there are alarming similarities between the
> attack on Lawrence and the My-Lai massacre, despite more
> than a century separating the two events. The parallel with
> this more recent American war is unavoidable, subtly empha-
> sized by the revelation at the end of the film that Jake is still
> only nineteen years old, often given as the average age of the
> American soldier in Vietnam. Lee's film seems to be saying
> that there is a disturbing, timeless facet to the American char-
> acter that is drawn only towards prejudice and destruction. It
> is a narrative theme almost unthinkable to pre-Vietnam Civil
> War melodramas that strive instead to emphasize unity in
> the American national family. Here the narrative consciously
> states that there are dangerous individuals who do not uphold
> positive values of mainstream American ideology.[11]

Whatever the positives and negatives about *Ride with the
Devil* and *Cold Mountain,* it must be said that both films—one
from a director born in Taiwan and one from a director born
in the United Kingdom—paint a grim picture of the official and
unofficial violence unleashed before, during, and after the Civil

War. While both films, because of their emphasis on the Southern participation in the war, cannot avoid openly or covertly falling prey to some of the myths of the Lost Cause, they also expose, on the other hand, so many of the lies of that series of fantasies and make an honorable attempt to include a more realistic view of the South.

7 "A Gallant Soldier and a Christian Gentleman"

The Reconciliation of North and South

—Well … the prodigal brother … Haven't seen you since the surrender.

—(*The Searchers*, 1956)

SMOKING THE PEACE PIPE

The United States Army had two missions in the post-Civil War era—to ensure the success of Reconstruction in the South and to pacify the Western frontier. Regarding Reconstruction, the army played three roles: (1) in 1865 to 1866 it supervised the restoration of loyal state governments in the South; (2) beginning in 1867, it implemented the Congressional plan of Reconstruction that reversed the earlier policy of restoration; and (3) until 1877, it engaged in a limited and erratic counter-insurgency operation to preserve "law and order" in the South. Although some officers were former abolitionists and supported Radical Reconstruction, many others had no sympathy with Radical policies or with the freedmen. Nevertheless, the federal government called on the army, as in the cases of Vietnam, Iraq, and Afghanistan, to engage in "nation building."[1] The famous Seventh Cavalry, for example, was recalled for the West three times during Reconstruction to restore order in Louisiana.

The army's role on the frontier was that of an agent of nation building—preparing the West beyond the Mississippi for exploitation by farmers, gold miners, railroads, and other agents of territorial expansion. Soldiers in the post-Civil War years established and protected the new Southern state governments and patrolled the western frontier.[2] Its ranks included immigrants, freedmen, and ex-Confederates. Out West, ex-rebels and their former Yankee opponents joined in the fight against the Plains Indians and other native American tribes. It was hard, low-paid duty and the desertion rate was high, except among black soldiers. Not surprisingly, Hollywood's history of the West ignored the role of African-American troopers and focused instead on white cavalrymen, especially, in the case of John Ford, on Irish immigrants and ex-Confederate recruits.

Other western films (parallel with the cavalry-to-the-rescue genre) glorified the ex-rebel, usually a reluctant gunslinger, as a loner seeking escape from war and defeat, but maintaining his Southern pride and allegiance to Southern values (none of which it seems had anything to do with slavery).

The reconciliation theme had appealing dramatic possibilities for the movie studios, but the movie makers did not invent the idea. The movies reflected a concept that had become central to the mystic memory of the Civil War. The war in American popular memory (except among African Americans) was not about slavery. It was about states' rights. (This became the common wisdom despite the fact that a goodly number of veterans on both sides undoubtedly continued to believe long after the fighting ended that the war was indeed about slavery.) The South fought bravely and honorably against overwhelming odds. Thus, the war came to be seen as an honorable contest that allowed historical memory to avoid the messy issue of race. It was all very romantic and, ultimately, the defeat of the South preserved a Union, something that all, ex-rebels as well as Yankees, could take pride in. Reconstruction, however, was "the tragic era." After the war, according to this interpretation, vengeful Radicals imposed an unjust peace on the South. The proud people of Dixie had to endure the oppression of carpetbaggers, scalawags, and ignorant freedmen until they were overthrown. The Klan was an unfortunate necessity, but short-lived. The tragic era came to an end as well, because Northerners,

now in sympathy with the South, allowed the decent white people of the South control of their own affairs. Shortly, the Civil
War became the "Brothers War"—a war in which both sides,
the interpretation held, fought for equally compelling and valid
"principles" (states' rights v. the Union). This was a key element
in the reconciliation theme—and in Hollywood's cavalry films.
The "Brothers" interpretation informed the dominant Civil War
narrative into the twentieth-first century; like radiation, it had
a long half-life.

"ENEMIES NO LONGER," 1913

Reconciliation as a theme in western films is predated by actual
reconciliation celebrations. Ancient film footage survives of the
reconciliation moments between the former foes as they "honor"
the fiftieth anniversary of the great battle and join hands. Although black troops did not fight at Gettysburg, not a single
black veteran was invited to participate in the ceremonies. Reconciliation was a white matter. The real issue of the war, slavery, was ignored along with the contributions of 180,000 black
soldiers. Reconciliation, minus African Americans, brought the
antagonisms, the war of competing "principles," to an end. In
an address to the assembled crowd, on July 4, 1913, President
Woodrow Wilson put the antagonism to rest: The old rivalry
gave way to nostalgia as former enemies reunited—it was the
birth of a nation: "We have found one another again as brothers and comrades in arms, enemies no longer, generous friends
rather, our battles long past, the quarrel forgotten—except that
we shall not forget the splendid valor."

In commemoration of the reunion, the New York Monuments
Commission issued a pamphlet recording the event. It wrote this
about "The Great Celebration":

> To those who were fortunate enough to be at the Reunion,
> there will remain always a deep and lasting impression of the
> affectionate relations between the Northern and Southern

veterans as they walked in close embrace and renewed their vows to honor and protect the preserved and united country: one flag, one home, one destiny.[3]

"THAT'S THE REBEL YELL," 1938

There was a second reconciliation celebration in July 1938, the seventy-fifth anniversary of the battle. By then, the 53,407 white veterans who attended the "Peace Jubilee" now numbered only 1,800. The official program for the events emphasized that is was "the final joint reunion of the Blue and the Gray." On the old battlefield, "these heroic figures will assemble in reunion ... there to mingle as friends." Such was the dominant narrative. Ironically, the rebel cause (disunion) was now alloyed to a new American nationalism: "Yes, the Veterans will want to recount significant incidents of their war service—they may want to swap yarns, smoke the peace pipe ... and, in general, have a hale-fellow-well met good time."[4]

The old veterans now appeared on film to record the reenact of Pickett's Charge where the Union survivors come out from cover to embrace the *slowly* charging Confederates. Two small groups of men face each other across a stone wall, shaking hands vigorously and saying, "Hello, hello" over and over again. One man turns to the camera and lets out a scream: "That's the Rebel Yell," he tells us in an aside. A modern overlay on the scene declares that these men constitute "The Other Greatest Generation." More shaking hands, more embraces. Uninvited and unseen in 1913, a handful of blacks, Union veterans, appear briefly. President Roosevelt addresses the gathering in a "spirit of brotherhood and peace." He accepts, for the country, the gift of the "Eternal Light Peace Memorial."

FROM BATTLEFIELD TO BACK LOT

American westerns, in particular the films set in the1860s and 1870s (contemporaneous with the history of Reconstruction), are frequently the vehicles for "reconciliation" scenes between former Civil War antagonists.

Consider how Hollywood bought into the pro-Southern myths of Reconstruction stories about heroic ex-rebels (the "unconquered" and unreconstructed) on the frontier West. These films reflected how the North, tired of the Southern insurgency and lacking an enduring commitment to black rights, abandoned the cause of Reconstruction. This abandonment can be explained in part by the spirit of "reconciliation"—the coming together of white Union and Confederate veterans in a spirit of nationalism, shared valor, and honorable service at the expense of the commitment to black rights in the South.

The Searchers (1956), for example, embodies these themes in the persona of Ethan Edwards (John Wayne), an embittered ex-Confederate soldier who returns to his brother's home in Texas in 1868 three years after the end of the war. He has not beaten his sword into a ploughshare as so many former combatants on both sides have done. His racism that apparently drove him into the Southern cause to begin with is now turned against Native Americans—all of them—but especially the Comanche who destroy his family and plunges him into a five-year search for his kidnapped niece. If Ethan Edwards remains unrepentant, Ford was much more supportive of reconciliation in his earlier "Cavalry Trilogy"—*Fort Apache* (1948), *She Wore a Yellow Ribbon* (1949), and *Rio Grande* (1950). Here the post-Civil War Union cavalry, now fighting a new enemy—the Native Americans—is a mixture of Northerners (many Union Army veterans) and Southerners (all Confederate Army veterans) who have put aside their former enmity to face a common foe—the Indians.

These themes of reconciliation can also be seen in works such as Ford's *Stagecoach* (1939), Sam Peckinpah's *Major Dundee* (1965), Andrew McLaglen's *The Undefeated* (1969), and Clint Eastwood's *The Outlaw Josey Wales* (1976), among many others, both "A" westerns and "B" westerns. There were TV westerns as well, including *The Rebel,* starring Nick Adams as a former Confederate soldier haunted by his memories of the Civil War. In the theme song to the series:

> He searched the land,
> This restless lad,
> He was panther quick and leather tough
> Cause he had figured that he'd been pushed enough, the rebel.

Hollywood pictured the ex-rebels sympathetically as tough loners and defenders of the underdogs on the frontier—the small farmer, the widow, and the immigrant. In a classic scene in *Shane* (1953), a sadistic gunfighter (Jack Wilson) goads a hapless, but proud ex-Confederate farmer from Alabama ("Stonewall" Torrey) into a gunfight and kills him:

Scene: A desolate frontier town
(filmed near Jackson Hole, Wyoming)

Wilson [Jack Palance]
They tell me they call you "Stone-wall."

Torrey [Elisha Cooke, Jr.]
Anything wrong with that?

Wilson
It's just funny. I guess they named a lot of that …
Southern trash after old Stonewall.

Torrey
Who'd they name you after? Or would you know?

Wilson
I'm saying that "Stonewall" Jackson was trash himself.
Him and Lee, and all the rest of them Rebs. You, too.

Torrey
You're a low-down, lying Yankee.

Wilson
Prove it.

(Torrey draws his gun, but Wilson is faster.)

Later, Shane, a gunfighter with a mysterious past, kills Wilson in retaliation; the insult to the memory of Southern heroes is revenged.

RECONCILIATION ON THE WESTERN FRONTIER: *STAGECOACH*

The Lost Cause myths played out in many formats and many genres, some of the most memorable versions coming in western films—once the most popular of all American films. In 1939, the same year as *Gone with the Wind,* John Ford's *Stagecoach,* one of the most enjoyable and, more importantly, one of the most influential films ever made in America, was released. When John Wayne made *The Searchers* in 1956, he had become "JOHN WAYNE." In 1939, he was still "John Wayne," known mainly for a string of 1930s' "B" westerns. By casting him as "Ringo Kid," Ford began the process that turned him into an icon. But the Lost Cause myths and the Unfinished Civil War are *not* embodied in Wayne's character as they are in *The Searchers.* The Civil War is refought—so to speak—by two other characters: a drunken Doctor from the North and a degenerated Cavalier from the South. Dr. Josiah Boone and Hatfield (no first name) find themselves fellow passengers on the stagecoach from Tonto to Lordsburg (in Arizona) for two different reasons. Doc Boone has been kicked out of town for drunkenness and for being unable to pay his bills. Hatfield, a gambler (and gunfighter?) voluntarily leaves town as the protector of Lucy Mallory, a genteel Southern woman representing every cliché about genteel Southern women, who is on her way to meet her husband, a Captain in the US Army. Hatfield, as we later learn, knows Lucy Mallory but she has no idea who he is. In the midst of a card game, he looks out of the window, sees her, and declares she is "Like an angel in a jungle." When one of the card players asks what he is talking about, Hatfield replies: "You wouldn't understand, cowboy. You've never seen an angel. Or a gentlewoman."

Geronimo has jumped the reservation and the stagecoach might be vulnerable to attack. Thus, Hatfield's decision to "protect" Mrs. Mallory. The Civil War is refought early on the journey as Doc Boone mentions that he once set the broken arm of Ringo's brother.

Boone: Let's see. I'd just been honorably discharged from the Union Army after the *War of the Rebellion* [our italics].

Hatfield: You mean the *War for the Southern Confederacy*, suh [our italics].

Boone: I mean nothing of the kind, sir.

In three lines of dialogue, *Stagecoach* crystallizes the unbending conflict in its most elemental form. Later, the verbal battle restarts as Boone's cigar smoke upsets Mrs. Mallory. An apologetic Boone tosses the cigar out of the window.

Boone: Being so partial to the weed myself, I forget it disagrees with others.

Hatfield: A gentleman doesn't smoke in the presence of a lady.

Boone: Three weeks ago I took a bullet out of a man who was shot by a gentleman ... The bullet was ... in his back.

So much for the cavalier tradition from a Yankee perspective. Later Doc Boone orates that he is not afraid to continue the journey even with the possibility of running into Geronimo whom he had earlier referred to as a "butcher."

Boone: I have always courted danger. During the late war ... when I had the honor, sir, to serve the union under our great President Abraham Lincoln and General Phil Sheridan, I fought midst shot and shell and the cannons' roar ...

He leaves off at this point to demand another drink.

Hatfield, for his part, finally gives Mrs. Mallory some hint of his concern for her:

Mrs. Mallory:	"You're very kind ... Why?"
Hatfield:	In the world I live in one doesn't often see a lady, Mrs. Mallory. [He added, in a line cut from the film, "I'm only doing my duty as a Southern gentleman."]
Lucy:	Have you ever been in Virginia?
Hatfield:	I was in your father's regiment.
Lucy:	I should remember your name. You're Mr ... Hatfield?
Hatfield:	That's what I'm called, yes.

Obviously "Hatfield" is the name taken at the end of the war along with his decision not to return to Virginia. That Hatfield is someone else, someone from "old Virginia," is confirmed when Mrs. Mallory asks for a drink of water. A canteen is offered. The script describes what comes next:

Hatfield takes the canteen from Ringo and pours some of the water into a small silver cup, then passes it to Lucy. Lucy takes the cup from Hatfield's outstretched hand and gracefully drinks. Then she closes its little lid and looks at it. She looks again, more closely, scrutinizing its *crest* and Latin inscription: "*ad astra per aspera*" as if trying to recall something from memory. She then looks up at Hatfield and leans forward, pointing to the cup as she questions him.

Lucy:	Haven't I seen this crest before? Isn't this from Ringfield Manor [a plantation home]?
Hatfield:	I wouldn't know, Mrs. Mallory. I won that cup on a wager.

In the end, Hatfield proves that some idea of how a Virginia cavalier behaves still resides in him. The stagecoach is attacked by Geronimo and his bloodthirsty Apaches and the defenders soon run out of ammunition. Hatfield sees that he has one bullet left in his pistol and prepares to shoot Mrs. Mallory in the head to keep her from falling into the hands of the savage Apaches. (Replicating a scene in *The Birth of a Nation* in which a white man prepares to put a bullet through the head of a white woman lest she be racially defiled.) But an Apache bullet stops him before he can pull the trigger and, simultaneously, the cavalry arrive to save the day.

Hatfield dies in the arms of Mrs. Mallory and, ironically, Doc Boone and his last words are the final revelation: "If you ever see Judge Ringfield ... (fighting for breath) ... tell him his son ..." One theme of the westerns, especially the ones set in the years soon after the Civil War, is the reconciliation of former enemies as they move from confronting each other to confronting new threats to Americans and America.

REBELS AND RACE: *THE SEARCHERS*

Scene: A Ranch House in the Middle of Monument Valley aka Texas, 1868

**Captain/Reverend Samuel Johnson Clayton
(Ward Bond) (expressing surprise at the sudden
appearance of Ethan Edwards (John Wayne)**
Well ... the prodigal brother ... Haven't seen you since
the surrender. (Pause) Come to think of it, I didn't see
you *at* the surrender.

Ethan Edwards
I don't believe in surrenderin' ... I still got my saber, Reverend ... never turned into any ploughshare neither!

The exchange between Clayton and Edwards, from John Ford's deeply powerful but deeply flawed film, indicates one of the ways that the Civil War still raged, especially in the hearts and minds of some Southerners, after the war actually ended. Ethan Edwards, still wearing his Confederate gray topcoat three years after the end of the war, finally returns to his brother's Texas ranch after—it seems—a seven-year absence. Besides being a Southern loyalist,

Ethan apparently went to war because he was (and is) in love with his brother's wife—Martha—and in the first few scenes—before she is raped and murdered by Comanche warriors—her facial expressions, body language, and tremulous voice strongly suggest that she loves in return. Asked about California, Edwards indicates he never went there. He did go to Mexico, fighting as a mercenary for the Emperor Maximilian. He has returned with a medal made of solid gold and two pouches filled with twenty dollar gold pieces. The exchange with Captain Clayton (of the Texas Rangers) takes place soon after his return when Clayton and a few others arrive to pursue thieves who have stolen a neighbor's cattle. Clayton tries to temporarily deputize Ethan's brother Aaron so he can join the posse but Edwards declares he will take his brother's place and that his brother should "stay close" to the ranch house because the thieves may be rustlers or they may be (and it turns out they are) a band of Comanche bent on a "murder raid." Switching brothers leads to another exchange emphasizing Ethan's loyalty to the South (and, by his words, to the Lost Cause).

Clayton (grudgingly):	All right ... I'll swear you in ...
Edwards:	You can forget that ... (as Sam stares) Wouldn't be legal anyway.
Clayton:	Why ... (a pause ... then shrewdly) ... You wanted for a crime, Ethan.

[Note: the script adds "Martha waits—intent"—one could add even fearful of the answer.]

Edwards:	You askin' as a Reverend or a Captain, Sam?
Clayton:	I'm askin' as a Ranger of the sovereign state of Texas.
Edwards:	Got a warrant?
Clayton:	You fit a lot of descriptions.
Edwards (levelly):	*... I figger a man's only good for one oath at a time ... I took mine to the Confederate States of America ...* (he pauses—then) *... So did you, Reverend* [our italics].

This brief scene suggests many things about Ethan's character. There is no further mention of the Civil War in the film, nor for that matter of slavery (as can be expected), but whether because of the war alone or a combination of circumstances, Ethan is no Southern cavalier. On the other hand, just as war is the continuation of policy by other means, 1950s' westerns, especially the best of them like *The Searchers,* constitute a discussion of black and white relations by other means; in this case using Native Americans as stand-ins for blacks. *The Searchers* was released in 1956, two years after the Brown vs. Board of Education decision by the Supreme Court which declared segregated schools unconstitutional, a decision that set off legal, political, cultural, social, and *sexual* battles that still resonate today. The year 1956 was also the year of the Montgomery Bus Boycott that began at the end of 1955 and would stretch until the end of 1956. One could say a second *Reconstruction* was taking shape and the response to it, in many ways, would be just as brutal as the war on the first Reconstruction but, in the long run, fortunately, not successful.

Ethan is an unrepentant racist, a borderline psychopath who hates Indians, all Indians, especially the Comanche. One of the things that makes *The Searchers* so intriguing and such a gold mine of speculation for film historians, film critics, and filmmakers is the mysterious nature of Ethan Edwards's character. Despite his insane hated of the Comanche, he speaks their language and even knows their customs, down to their ideas about the afterlife, just as white Southerners, before and after the war, declared their intimate knowledge of how blacks thought and behaved. Most importantly, as an unrepentant Confederate, he is obsessed with the "abomination" of sexual contact between whites and, in this case, not blacks, but Indians. He and Thomas Dixon and D. W. Griffith view the world through the same sexually deranged eyes.

His sister-in-law, the love of his life is raped (and probably mutilated as well before being murdered) during the attack on his brother's home. His brother and nephew are also murdered but his two nieces—Lucy, about twenty and Debbie, about ten—are taken captive by the Comanche. Ethan, initially assisted by two others—his adopted "nephew" Martin Pauley who Edwards distrusts because he is one-eighth Cherokee and Brad Jorgenson who was courting Lucy—commence what becomes a five-year "search" to find Debbie. Lucy is found early in the search—also raped, mutilated, and murdered—by Ethan who wraps her body in his Confederate topcoat and buries her "with my own hands." At first he withholds the information from Brad and Martin but he has to reveal the truth because Brad thinks he has found Lucy. At a distance he saw her "blue dress."

Edwards: What you saw was a buck wearin' Lucy's dress ... I thought it best to keep it from you—long as I could.
Brad: Did they ...? Was she ...?
Edwards (Ethan wheels on him in shouting fury): What've I got to do—draw you a picture? ... Spell it out? ... Don't ever ask me! ... Long as you live don't ever ask me more!

Moments later, Brad is dead as his grief impels him to attack the three or four Comanche, including the one wearing Lucy's dress. The search continues, one year becomes two years, eventually becomes five years. Ethan and Martin make one visit "home" to the Jorgensen ranch a year after Brad's death. Ethan is determined to continue the search but suggests that Martin stay behind to work for Brad's father, especially since Brad's sister Laurie insists that she and Martin have been "going steady" since they were three years old! But Martin sees the need to continue as well. Something has gone wrong with Ethan and Martin fears for Debbie when and if they ever find her. "That's what scares me—him findin' her ... Laurie, I've seen his eyes when he so much as hears the word 'Comanche' ... I've seen him take his knife an' ... never mind ... But he's a man can go crazy wild ..." That's as far as he gets in the film. But the original script indicates he continues: "It might come on him when it was the worst thing could be ... What I counted on, I hoped to be there to stop him, if such a thing come." And, as the years pass, Ethan becomes "crazy wild" more often. Once when they stop to kill a buffalo for meat, Ethan shoots one buffalo after another. Martin asks "What's the sense in it?" and Ethan (in a fury) replies: "Hunger!—Empty bellies! That's the sense of it, you Cherokee! ..." Ethan keeps firing until the herd runs off and then adds "Least, *they* won't feed any Comanche this winter ... Killin' buffalo's as good as killin' Injuns in this country." Later they enter an Army camp after the cavalry has destroyed a Comanche village and brought back several white girl captives. Every one of them is deranged in some way as the film suggests that living with the Comanche has driven them insane. Ethan and Martin walk among them, hoping to find Debbie but with no luck. A soldier says to Ethan: "Hard to realize they're white." Ethan replies: "They're not white any more—they're Comanche!" Ford emphasizes the hatred that this idea festers in Ethan by having his camera dolly in for a tight close-up of Ethan's face, seething with unspoken rage.

After four years or more into the search, they finally find Debbie, now about fifteen, and living in the tent of Comanche chief "Scar," who led the attack that destroyed her family, as one of his "wives." Ethan and Martin camp nearby, uncertain as to what Scar will do since he obviously knows who they are and why they are there. Suddenly Debbie comes to them, begging them to leave because the Comanche are now "her people." In the original version of the script, she defends the Comanche saying they saved her when her family was attacked by white rustlers, but Martin starts to convince her of this lie. In the film version, she tells Martin that she remembers him "from always" and prayed for him to find her but it is now too late. At this point Ethan draws his pistol with the intention of killing her. Martin stands in front of her to protect her and only a sudden attack by Scar and his warriors prevents Ethan from killing her (and perhaps Martin as well). Ethan is wounded in the attack and, after they escape, writes a will in which he leaves all his property to Martin because he has no living kin. Martin flings the document back in Ethan's face with, "You can keep your will! I ain't forgotten' you was all set to shoot her yourself ... What kind of a man are you, anyway." Ethan's reply, again, could have come straight from one of Dixon's novels: "She's been with bucks! She's nothing' now but a ..." Imagine what word or words follow that "a"!

Martin shouts back: "Shut your dirty mouth!" So Debbie has been irreversibly "tainted." Unlike Flora, she doesn't choose to kill herself so someone, her uncle, must do it for her ... for her sake and for the sake of whites in general.

Near the end of the film after Scar's camp is located, Captain Clayton and the Rangers along with Ethan and some cavalrymen plan an attack to try to rescue Debbie. Laurie asks Martin not to go. It seems, from her reply, that Ethan's sexual obsession with race is not confined to him.

Laurie:	It's too late ... She's a woman grown now.
Martin:	I got to fetch her home.
Laurie:	Fetch *what* home? ... The leavin's of Comanche bucks ... sold time an' again to the highest bidder? ... With savage brats of her own, most like?
Martin (shouting it):	*Laurie!* Shut your mouth!
Laurie:	Do you know what Ethan will do if he has a chance? ... He'll put a bullet in her brain! And I tell you Martha would want him to!
Martin:	Only if I'm dead!

(Scar's camp is seen in the pre-dawn light and the Rangers prepare to charge in and attack.)

Wait! We go chargin' in, they'll kill her ... and you know it.

Ethan (calmly):	It's what I'm countin' on.
Martin:	I know you are ... Only it ain't goin' to be that way ... she's alive ...
Ethan:	Livin' with Comanches ain't bein' alive ...
Martin:	She's alive ... Better she's alive and livin' with Comanches than her brains bashed out ...

Martin eventually prevails and is allowed to try to sneak into the camp to find Debbie and get her out. But Captain Clayton makes no promises once the shooting starts: "... at the first alarm, we're comin' in—and we ain't goin' to have time to pick and choose our targets when we do …"

Martin finds Debbie and kills Scar. The Rangers charge in (the script specifically saying that Clayton leads them in shouting the "Rebel yell") and Martin runs away from the campsite with Debbie to save her. Ethan sees them, pursues them, and knocks Martin down. He confronts Debbie and prepares to shoot her. In the original script, he looks down at her and says, "You sure favor your mother." He then picks her up; his racial and sexual rage apparently purged by the memory of his beloved Martha. In the film, he picks her up, stares at her for a moment, then cradles her in his arms and says, "Let's go home Debbie." By making Ethan's change of heart less specific, Ford retains the "mystery" of Ethan's character to the very end. After five years of seething, murderous rage and sexual obsession, there is no explanation for his decision not to kill Debbie. *The Searchers* ends with one of the most memorable moments in the history of film. Martin and Laurie are reunited; Debbie is taken into the Jorgensen house; family has been restored. But Ethan Edwards, the unrepentant Confederate who returned to his brother's home five years earlier seemingly seeking reintegration into family and community, now stands alone and solitary *outside* the Jorgensen house; he walks *slowly* away, as the door *slowly* closes, accepting perpetual exile.

We have spent these pages discussing *The Searchers* in detail because the closer one looks at the film, the more it actually emerges as something more than a typical John Ford western (if there actually is one). *The Searchers* replays, in the ways detailed above, an enormous number of the Lost Cause and Unfinished Civil War themes. And *The Searchers* is not the only western film that plays out these themes.

THEMES PLAYED AND REPLAYED IN FILM

One theme of the westerns, especially the ones set in the years soon after the Civil War, is the reconciliation of former enemies as they move from confronting each other to confronting new threats to

Americans and America. Seven years before *The Searchers,* John Ford, in the second of his "Cavalry Trilogy," *She Wore a Yellow Ribbon* (1949), injects a poignant moment of reconciliation into the film. An older soldier known as "Private John Smith" is mortally wounded in a battle with rampaging dog soldiers. Sergeant Tyree (Ben Johnson), who refers to his commander as a "Yankee officer," calls to Captain Nathan Brittles (John Wayne) to "take a look at Trooper Smith." "Dixie" plays softly on the soundtrack with the sound of a harp most prominent:

Trooper John Smith (as he dies):	Don't bother about me, Captain. Trust you'll forgive my presumption … I'd like to recommend the boy here … for the way he handled the action. In the very best tradition of the cavalry, sir.
Tyree (to Smith):	I take that very kindly, sir.
Smith:	*Captain Tyree! Captain Tyree!* [our italics]
Brittles:	Speak to him.
Tyree:	Thank you. (Comes to attention.) Yes, Sir. Sir! Sir!
Brittles:	(realizing that Smith has died): I'm afraid he can't hear you, Captain.

So who was Private John Smith and why was he calling Sergeant Tyree "Captain"? The little matter of the Civil War being over, both Smith and Tyree (ex-rebels) have reconciled with the Union Army, and, yet, retained the old allegiance—an allegiance recognized even by their "Yankee" commanding officer.

Brittles (later, while burying Smith):	I also commend to your keeping the soul of Rome Clay, late Brigadier General, Confederate States of America. Known to his comrades here, Sir, as Trooper John Smith, United States cavalry … a gallant soldier and a Christian gentleman.

Following the ceremony, Tyree places a small rebel battle flag on the coffin. "The Battle Hymn of the Republic" accompanies other scenes in the film when Wayne's character is set to retire from the service. Later, when Brittles receives an unexpected post-retirement appointment as Chief of Scouts for the army, he tells Tyree that the letter is endorsed by Phil Sheridan, William Tecumseh Sherman and U.S. Grant. Tyree observes that it would be even better if the appointment carried the signature of Robert E. Lee. Brittle agrees.

Reconciliation also is a factor in the other two films of the Ford "Cavalry Trilogy." In *Fort Apache,* John Wayne, beloved U.S. cavalry officer, was a colonel in the Confederate army. In *Rio Grande,* John Wayne is a US cavalry officer from the North but his estranged wife—Maureen O'Hara—with whom he *reconciles* by the end of the film—is from the South.

Three other films from the 1960s and 1970s, among many other "A" and "B" westerns, also deal with the post-Civil War theme of reconciliation mixed with ongoing enmities that still simmer: *Major Dundee* (1965), *The Undefeated* (1969), and *The Outlaw Josey Wales* (1976).

Version One: *Major Dundee*

Major Dundee, directed by Sam Peckinpah (during one of his self-destructive periods), features Charlton Heston and Richard Harris as former West Point comrades who ended up on opposite sides during the war. Ben Tyreen (Harris) has a long standing grudge against Amos Dundee (Heston) because Dundee cast the deciding vote in Tyreen's court-martial for participation in a duel (as any Southern cavalier would do; it's genetically coded). Dundee has been reassigned to New Mexico after some vaguely described mistakes that he made at Gettysburg. Rampaging Apaches under a bloodthirsty chief (are there any other kind?) named Sierra Charriba are massacring ranchers and cavalry. Dundee assembles his own "army" of Union troops, both black and white, Confederate prisoners, led by Tyreen, Indian scouts, and civilian mercenaries to pursue Charriba into Mexico. Despite his animosity towards Dundee, Tyreen agrees to serve the mission loyally but "only" until Charriba is "killed or taken."

The disaster that *Major Dundee* turned into (although a Sam Peckinpah "disaster" still means it is better than most other directors' "triumphs") is a subject for film historians. The emphasis here is on the continuation of the Civil War antagonisms, which are maintained throughout a good portion of the film. When one of Tyreen's men tries to desert, he is captured and Dundee announces that he will be hanged. Tyreen objects but Dundee is adamant so Tyreen shoots the man rather than see a loyal Confederate "hung" by a Yankee. A black Union soldier Aesop (Brock Peters), the leader of the black troops, gets into a fight with one of Tyreen's men, Jimmy Lee Benteen (John Davis Chandler), a belligerent racist.

Once in Mexico, Dundee's force not only has to deal with Charriba but also French troops loyal to Emperor Maximilian (the very same person who awarded Ethan Edwards with a solid gold medal) whose supplies they steal to replenish their own. Eventually, Charriba is tricked into attacking what appears to be a weakened and vulnerable Dundee force and he and his Apache warriors are wiped out. As they approach the Rio Grande river to cross back into the United States, they are confronted by a contingent of French troops. As the battle develops, Tyreen is shot. He seizes the *American* flag and, as he is dying, delays the arrival of additional French troops so that Dundee and the other survivors can make it across the river.

Version Two: *The Undefeated*

Four years later Andrew McLaglen and John Wayne (uncredited) directed *The Undefeated* with John Wayne as Union Colonel John Henry Thomas and Rock Hudson as Confederate Colonel James Langdon. Thomas had defeated Langdon in a battle, only to learn the war had ended a few days before. Unrepentant, Langdon defiantly burns down his plantation; he and his men plan to cross into Mexico to join the forces of Emperor Maximilian (and perhaps run into Ethan Edwards!). Simultaneously, Thomas, his adopted Indian son Blue Boy, and his surviving troops bring a herd of 3,000 horses into Mexico to sell in Durango.

Halfway to Durango, Blue Boy, using his Indian cunning, realizes that bandits are planning to attack a group of travelers, who turn out to be Langdon and his followers. Thomas and *his* men rescue the Confederates and drive off the bandits. The two groups of former enemies celebrate at a party that takes place conveniently, for the theme of the film, on the Fourth of July. Everyone has a good time and the war is bloodlessly refought in a series of fistfights between the two sides. Could it be more obvious that McLaglen (and Wayne) were trying to make a John Ford film without John Ford. *The Undefeated* is clearly the weakest of the three films discussed here.

The two groups go their separate ways but Blue Boy and Langdon's daughter have fallen in love (a good thing Ethan Edwards wasn't on the scene). Langdon and his group are captured by a Mexican general who will release them in exchange for Thomas's horses. Seeming to agree, Thomas stampedes his herd through the Mexican camp to rescue the hostages. North and South unite, once again, to put aside old hatreds and to defeat a common enemy. Notice in both *Major Dundee* and *The Undefeated*, the enemy is both foreign and located in a foreign country: Apaches and French in the former; Mexicans in the latter.

Version Three: *The Outlaw Josey Wales*

The Outlaw Josey Wales, directed by Clint Eastwood, is the most successful of these films. Eastwood is Wales, a "peaceful" Missouri farmer and unreconstructed Southerner who seeks revenge for the brutal murder of his wife and son by pro-Union Kansas "Redlegs" (as Union sympathizers were called) led by Captain Terrill (Bill McKinney), a protégé of the infamous Senator James H. Lane (shades of *Ride with the Devil* two decades later). Wales joins the Missouri Bushwackers/Border Ruffians. At the end of the war, the guerrillas are persuaded to surrender with a promise of amnesty. Wales, still seeking revenge, refuses to surrender, thus surviving the massacre of the men by a band of "Redlegs" who are now part of the Union army. Wales manages to shoot down several of the attackers with a Gatling gun. Senator Lane offers a $5,000,000 reward for Wales who is now on the run from the Union Army and bounty hunters while still seeking revenge and trying to get to Texas to start anew. He takes along a wounded survivor of the massacre, Jamie (Sam Bottoms).

On the run, he acquires a "new" family in the form of an old Cherokee named Lone Watie (Chief Dan George), a young Navajo woman (Geraldine Kearns), an elderly woman from Kansas (Paula Trueman), and her granddaughter who has been rescued from a band of Comanches (Sondra Locke, and her name is Laura Lee, not Debbie Edwards!). Cornered by the Redlegs in their new "home" in Texas, the "family" fights back and wins. Wales kills Captain Terrill, the leader of the Redlegs, who had ordered the massacre of the guerrillas, with his own US cavalry sword. Wales manages to convince all but one of his pursuers that he has been killed in Monterrey, Mexico by five gunmen. The one skeptic declares that he will go to Mexico himself to look for Wales. The film ends on that note. Wales has purged himself of his hatred and will be reborn as family man.

Of the three films, *Wales* was the most critically and financially successful and that success came at a time—the 1970s—when the western was in serious decline. In an interview Eastwood called *Wales* an anti-war film:

> As for Josey Wales, I saw the parallels to the modern day at that time. Everybody gets tired of it, but it never ends. A war is a horrible thing, but it's also a unifier of countries … Man becomes his most creative during war … But that's a kind of sad statement on mankind if that's what it takes.[5]

RECONCILIATION AND REUNION, 1961

In 1961, the nation had once again an opportunity to celebrate the reconciliation of North and South—the Centennial of the

American Civil War. But, as the website of the National Archives and Records Administration notes:

> Congress created a Civil War Centennial Commission that sponsored and encouraged activities to commemorate the war's 100th anniversary—including battle reenactments, conferences, publications, costume balls, and exhibits. The events emphasized the bravery of the soldiers from both sides and national reconciliation after the war. They largely ignored the political and economic causes of the conflict, slavery, African Americans, and postwar violence against blacks.[6]

So, the anniversary was not about the thing that actually caused the war or the people the war had liberated; rather, it was about shared glory and the birth of a nation. In the 1961 *Civil War Centennial Handbook,* the caption under a photograph of Confederate and Union veterans shaking hands reads: "They have become a common property and a common responsibility of the American people."[7]

8 The Princess of the Moon

The Lost Cause, Reconstruction, and Southern Memory

For every Southern boy fourteen years old, not once but whenever he wants it, there is the instant when it's still not yet two o'clock on that July afternoon in 1863, the brigades are in position behind the rail fence, the guns are laid and ready in the woods and the furled flags are already loosened to break out and Pickett himself with his long oiled ringlets and his hat in one hand probably and his sword in the other looking up the hill waiting for Longstreet to give the word and it's all in the balance, it hasn't happened yet, it hasn't even begun yet, it not only hasn't begun yet but there is still time for it not to begin against that position and those circumstances which made more men than Garnett and Kemper and Armistead and Wilcox look grave yet it's going to begin, we all know that, we have come too far with too much at stake and that moment doesn't need even a fourteen-year-old boy to think This time. Maybe this time with all this much to lose and all this much to gain: Pennsylvania, Maryland, the world, the golden dome of Washington itself to crown with desperate and unbelievable victory.

(William Faulkner, *Intruder in the Dust*, 1948)

THE LOST CAUSE CATECHISM

In its fully developed form the Lost Cause catechism taught four essential doctrines: 1) antebellum Southerners created a strong sense of community—white and black people exhibited mutual dependence, respect, even affection; 2) the South fought a just war for states' rights (not slavery) against an aggressive, hypocritical North; 3) the Confederacy was defeated only because of the Union's superior numbers and resources; and 4) Southern soldiers fought honorably and bravely to the bitter end.[1]

Accompanying the core beliefs were a pantheon of saints, including Robert E. Lee, "Stonewall" Jackson, and Jefferson Davis, in one case literally chiseled in rock—the Stone Mountain, Georgia memorial, a Confederate Mount Rushmore. The images of Davis, Lee, and Jackson are 90 × 100 feet, recessed 42 feet in the side of the mountain. Conceived in 1912 by a member of the Daughters of the Confederacy, the project was not fully completed until 1972. In 1914, an editorial in the *Atlanta Georgian* predicted that the images would rival the Pyramids, the Roman Coliseum, and the great bronze Buddha of Kamakura. The carving would honor "the great cause fought without shame and lost without dishonor."[2] Today the monument has been incorporated into a popular theme park with steamboat rides, nature walks, an evening laser show, and, of course, the inevitable gift-shop souvenirs—the image of Davis, Lee, and Jackson embossed on refrigerator magnets, mouse pads, and coffee mugs.

In regard to this pseudo-theological aspect, Charles Reagan Wilson's *Baptized in Blood: The Religion of the Lost Cause, 1865–1920* recounts the apotheosis of the Confederate soldier. He evokes, for example, the grand celebration in 1872 in Richmond, Virginia at the time of the dedication of a monument to Thomas "Stonewall" Jackson. The city went all out to decorate the area around the monument. Here is a reporter's description of the Grand Arch honoring the memory of the Jackson, and by implication all of those who fought for the Confederacy:

> It was thirty-two feet high. It was constructed with two turreted towers covered with evergreen, with an arch connecting them. On the west side of the arch was inscribed in large letters. "Warrior, Christian, Patriot." Just above this

was a painting representing a stone-wall, upon which was resting a bare saber, a Bible, and Confederate cap, with the angel of peace ascending, pointing heavenward.[3]

THE PRINCESS OF THE MOON

Cora Semmes Ives's Confederate pedigree was impeccable. She was a Virginian and the wife of Colonel Joseph Christmas Ives, a colonel who served as aide-de-camp to Jefferson Davis's staff during the Civil War. She was also the sister of Thomas J. Semmes, a Confederate senator, and first cousin of Raphael Semmes, a famous rebel naval officer. In 1869 she published a fairy tale. Its purpose was to entertain and instruct the "little sufferers of the South" rendered homeless and destitute. These are "poor little wanderers from Atlanta and the children of burning of Columbia …" Here is the story:

Once upon a time "after the dreadful struggle between the North and South," a Confederate soldier sits beneath a tree contemplating with "bitter disappointment" the defeat of the South, the death of his father, and the blackened ruins of the family plantation. His name is Randolph. He recalls how "he had buckled on his sword in defense of his native land," and he remembers too "his mother's last embrace, his aged father's blessing, and his own promise to return and brighten their declining years with the laurels of victory and liberty." Now all is lost. At that instant the Fairy of the Moon appears. She offers him a white winged horse to transport him to the moon. As he flies over the earth he sees the conquered South—a "desolate land he could not gaze upon without tears, for he beheld misery and want in all directions." He also observes "the homes of the conquerors, abounding in plenty, and decked in the spoils they had so cruelly acquired."

Arriving on the moon, he discovers a "sublime land" of peaceful beauty: rare flowers, bright-colored birds, and luxuriant foliage, where "zephyrs made the most delightful music." There he meets the moon people, inhabitants of a utopian society, and falls in love with the Princess of the Moon. He tells her "the history of his life—describing the once happy and prosperous land of his birth; then the misery and ruin brought upon his beloved people by a dreadful war; last of all, his own despoiled home."

To win her hand Randolph has to meet a series of challenges that test his virtue. Later he is allowed to marry the princess. But the marriage ceremony is suddenly interrupted when Yankees, descending from hot air balloons, invade the lunar kingdom: "From these curiously shaped affairs floated banners of red and white stripes, and in a few minutes a number of individuals issued forth, carrying 'carpetbags' ..." The imperious travelers "seemed not the least disconcerted by the crowd of peaceful-looking people who gazed so wonderingly and calmly upon them. Indeed, they made themselves so much at home that they would have appeared to be the owners of this fair country and the natives the intruders." Randolph's faithful ex-slave has accompanied the Yankee astronauts. "God bless me!" he exclaims as he hugs his former owner. "If here ain't Massa at last, 'live and well arter all!"

Randolph explains to the startled moon people, who are taken aback by the "grimaces and contortions" of the odd being:

> this singular individual (pointing to the grinning darkey) was an old and trusted servant belonging to my father's household, and one to whom I am greatly attached. He heard that an expedition was forming to survey the moon, and having dreamed that he should find me here, he was induced to join the party in hopes of realizing his wishes. After setting out, he discovered that the adventurers were the very persons who had burned down and driven from my home my aged parents.

At this point, the good Fairy reappears to defend the moon, summoning dragons to defend the moon. The Yankees flee, dropping the silverware they had stolen from the hero's plantation. The Fairy calls out to the invaders:

> You may well rejoice that your captor, being a Confederate soldier, spurns to trample on fallen foes, even though

they be the pillagers and plunderers of his own house-hold. Repent your ways while you have time. A respite of punishment has been granted to enable you to return and warn your people against Nemesis, whose uplifted hand is ready to strike the blow that will carry destruction in its wake. Tell them to unshackle the race of heroes they have enslaved, that the temple of liberty may not be shattered and sow terror in their midst. Tell them to restore ill-gotten goods, and bring contentment to the sad hearts and plenty to the scanty boards of those whom they have ruined. Retri-bution's sword ... is suspended over them. Go avert the evil before it is too late.

The good Fairy waves her magic wand, clothes the hero in a splendid new Confederate uniform, and bestows on him a sword of honor: "Live hereafter in peace and happiness, and know that your fallen country will yet arise from her ashes in greater glory." The Confederate hero and the Princess of the Moon live happily ever after. The rapacious carpetbaggers return to earth—landing in New York City. They are last heard of selling balloon rides to newlyweds in Central Park.[4]

MAGIC THINKING AND THE LOST CAUSE

The story of Randolph and his Princess is imperfectly imagined; the writing is awkward. Whatever the conceptual and stylistic weaknesses inherent in the fairy tale, however, the story is reveal-ing in what it says about the real or imagined "sufferings of the Southern people" and their historical narrative. The fairy tale as metaphor reveals the magic thinking that turned Southern mili-tary defeat into a moral victory—shifting the burden of history from the shoulders of the Southerners to the Northerners and the newly freed slaves during the Reconstruction years. The war fought to protect a system of human slavery became the war for states' rights—a just war in defense of family and community. It became the War of Northern Aggression. The Southern struggle against Reconstruction became a struggle against oppression and corruption. The persistence of the Confederate interpretation of Civil War and Reconstruction history and the general acceptance in American historical memory of this interpretation are remarkable considering that the war had cost 750,000 lives and nearly destroyed the Union. How did this happen? How were the losers (the ex-rebels) able to impose their interpretation of the war and its aftermath on the historical record? How did they get to write the history? The answer lies in the history of the Myth of the Lost Cause and the appeal of the underdog in American culture.

Helping to promote and to maintain the "fairy tale," not of Confederates on the moon, but of victimization of the South, are the versions of the Lost Cause myths created in films, from the earliest one-and-two reelers to the three-hour color spectacle of *Gone with the Wind,* and beyond.

THE LITTLE COLONEL

The year 1935 saw the release of two films that continued to set everyone straight about the Civil War and its aftermath. Both films—*The Littlest Rebel* and *The Little Colonel*—starred the pint-sized juggernaut of American film: Shirley Temple (born 1928) who, even at age seven, appeared to have acting, singing, and dancing skills that bordered on the preternatural. *The Littlest Rebel* was discussed earlier in Chapter 2 where she and Abraham Lincoln have a memorable encounter.

The Little Colonel, made twenty years after the malignantly vile view of the Civil War and its aftermath presented in *The Birth of a Nation,* can be seen as a malignantly benign view of those events. It achieves reconciliation between North and South without the need for the Ku Klux Klan to terrorize the freedmen in order to establish white control everywhere in the South. The reconciliation within *The Little Colonel* is "personal" not "political" but, nevertheless, embodies several aspects of the myth. "Crusty" old Colonel Lloyd (Lionel Barrymore—talk about reconciliation; he switches sides to play "crusty" old Thaddeus Stevens seven years later in *Tennessee Johnson*), who never accepts challenges to his patriarchal authority, learns his daughter—Elizabeth—is in love with and preparing to elope with a Union officer. He vows to cut himself off completely if she does so. Father and daughter angrily go at each other and Elizabeth leaves to marry her "Yankee." Years later, Elizabeth, her husband Jack Sherman, and their daughter (Miss Lloyd Sherman)—Shirley Temple of course—return to rent a small house that belonged to Elizabeth's mother and which happens to be right next to "crusty" Colonel Lloyd himself. Grandfather and granddaughter meet accidently and enter into a series of clashes to determine which one is the most stubborn. It's obviously no contest. Little Miss Lloyd Sherman is invincible. When trouble descends on her parents in the form of two men trying to rob them of legal rights, the old Colonel comes to the rescue, pistols ready to protect his daughter and granddaughter and, once the villains have been turned over to the law, to, at last, form a reconciliation with Elizabeth and Miss Lloyd and even his "Yankee" son-in-law.

The "benign" aspect of the film resides, of course, in the depiction of the former slaves who are still faithful and loyal to the old Colonel. Hattie McDaniel, warming up for her "Mamie" role four years later in *Gone with the Wind,* is the happy, smiling, singing cook and housekeeper who tends to the old Colonel's needs and who, of course, instantly comes under Miss Lloyd's magic charm. Bill "Bojangles" Robinson, who appears in both *The Little Colonel* and *The Littlest Rebel,* dances and sings with Miss Lloyd with never a frown crossing his face.

Both *The Little Colonel* and *The Littlest Rebel* are charming pieces of entertainment; Shirley Temple remains the most extraordinary child actor, singer, and dancer the movies have ever seen. But the charm can only go so far. A closer look reveals the myth at work at every level in both films.

MEMORY LAPSES INTO SENILITY

Meanwhile, back in Georgia, the Southern (and Catholic) writer Flannery O'Connor puts a savagely sardonic twist on the memory of the Lost Cause in "A Late Encounter with the Enemy," written in 1953, and published as part of the short-story collection *A Good Man is Hard to Fi*nd (1955).

The story is ideal to consider at this point because the images on film, in photographs, in drawings, and in print of the "Peace Jubilee" emphasized, besides the endless embraces between the former enemies, the toll that time had taken on them all. In the film footage some seem barely conscious of where they are; some seem barely conscious. Watching the film makes one wonder if any of them actually could remember what they had experienced half a century before.

Robert Penn Warren, in his extended essay *The Legacy of the Civil War* (1961), states: "When one is happy in forgetfulness, facts get forgotten."[5] How the actual events of the Civil War, as opposed to the cultural industry's twisted history, can be lost in a fog of forgetfulness and thus open to myth-making or even outright fabrication is the subject of O'Connor's story that connects to the Civil War and its aftermath in memory. As in so much of her work, O'Connor mixes humor and cruelty together with powerful results. In many ways, O'Connor's story sits at the opposite ends of the fairy-tale spectrum from "The Princess of the Moon."

Major George Poker Sash is 104 years old, O'Connor tells us. He lives with his granddaughter Sally Poker Sash who, after twenty years of summer courses, is about to graduate from college. More than anything she wants her grandfather, known to the world as General Tennessee Flintlock Sash, to sit on the stage at her commencement ceremony:

> She wanted the General at her graduation because she wanted to show what she stood for, or, as she said "what all was behind her," and was not behind them. The *them* was not anyone in particular. It was just all the upstarts who had turned the world on its head and unsettled the ways of decent living.

Moreover, who better to represent the unturned and unsettled world than the epitome of traditional virtue and values, the Civil War hero, the repository of memory of better times? The General, in fact, has no objection to attending as long as he can sit on the stage.

> He liked to sit on any stage. He considered that he was still a very handsome man. When he had been able to stand up, he measured five feet four inches of pure game cock. He had white hair that reached to his shoulders behind and would not wear teeth because he thought his profile was more striking without them. When he put on his full-dress general's uniform, he knew well enough that there was nothing to match him anywhere.

The General, never actually a General, but became a "General" as a result of the ultimate cultural industry production about the Civil War, *Gone with the Wind*. He does not speak much anymore but "There was only one event in the past that had any significance for him or that he cared to talk about: ... when he received the general's uniform and had been in the premiere."

The film is never explicitly named, but what else can it be other than the film that premiered in Atlanta twelve years earlier. He went from being George Poker Sash to "General" Tennessee Flintlock Sash at the hands of a publicist for the film. He and Sally are invited to Atlanta and, before the premiere ceremonies,

> "I was in the preemie they had in Atlanta ... They gimme this uniform and they gimme this soward and they say, 'Now General ... All we want you to do is march right up on that stage when you're innerduced tonight and answer a few questions.'"

The General—almost—plays his part to perfection ("He was the hit of the show," according to Sally).

O'Connor, with that savage wit and irony that suffused her writing describes the scene and, in doing so, turns so many of the Lost Cause clichés on their head:

> The old man walked slowly up the aisle with his fierce white head high and his hat held over his heart. The orchestra began to play the Confederate Battle Hymn very softly and the UDC (United Daughters of the Confederacy) members rose as a group and did not sit down again until the General was on the stage. When he reached the center of the stage with Sally Poker just behind him guiding his elbow, the orchestra burst into a loud rendition of the Battle Hymn and the old man, with real stage presence, gave a vigorous trembling salute and stood at attention until the last blast had died away. Two of the usherettes in Confederate caps and short skirts held a *Confederate and a Union flag crossed behind them* [our italics].

When asked his age, the General screams "Niiiiiinntty-two!" Pretending to be impressed and amazed, the master of ceremonies addresses the audience: "'let's give the General the biggest hand we've got!'" and, to the General's chagrin, signals to Sally to get him off the stage as quickly as possible. But the General has something to say: will it be about the war, about its triumphs and tragedies, about his memories? "He elbowed his granddaughter roughly away. 'How I keep so young,' he screeched, 'I kiss all the pretty guls!'"

In fact, "pretty guls" seems to be the only thing the General now really remembers or cares about. With quiet brutality, O'Connor demolishes the theme of memory:

> He had not actually been a general in that war. He had probably been a foot soldier; he didn't remember what he had been; in fact he didn't remember the war at all ... He didn't remember the Spanish–American War in which he lost a son; he didn't even remember his son. He didn't have any use for history because he never expected to meet it again. To his mind, history was connected with processions and

life with parades and he liked parades. People were always asking him if he remembered this or that—a dreary black procession of questions about the past.

What the General remembers is "pretty guls" such as the ones who surrounded him at the premiere in Atlanta. If he had been alone with one in his hotel room in Atlanta, "'I'd a known what to do.'" So many beautiful guls from Hollywood had been there. "'They took my pitcher ... it was two of them. One on either side and me in the middle with my arms around each of them's waist and their waist ain't any bigger than half a dollar.'" He constantly thinks of processions with beautiful girls on floats. Even as he is dying, in the middle of Sally's graduation ceremony, among the images—past and present—that flood his mind is "himself and the horse mounted in the middle of a float full of beautiful girls ..."

The twelve years of his life between 92 and 104 have seen the General slowly deteriorate but not die. Again, O'Connor brutally and unsentimentally bulldozes the myths.

His feet were completely dead now, his knees worked like old hinges, his kidneys functioned when they would, but his heart persisted to beat. The past and the future were the same thing to him, one forgotten and the other not remembered; he had no more notion of dying than a cat. Every year on Confederate Memorial Day, he was bundled up and *lent* [our italics] to the Capitol City Museum where he was *displayed* [our italics] from one to four in a musty room full of old photographs, old uniforms, old artillery, and historic documents. All these were carefully preserved in glass cases so that children would not put their hands on them. He wore his general's uniform from the premiere and sat, with a fixed scowl, inside a small roped area. There was nothing about him to indicate that he was alive except an occasional movement in his milky gray eyes, but once when a bold child touched his sword, his arm shot forward and slapped the child off in an instant. In the spring when the old homes were opened for pilgrimages, he was invited to wear his uniform, sit in a conspicuous spot, and lend atmosphere to the scene. Some of the times he only snarled at the visitors but sometimes he told about the premiere and the beautiful girls.

As he prepares to sit on the stage for Sally's graduation, wearing his uniform, he demands that Sally "Put the soward across my lap, dam you ... where it'll shine." Actually, he has no idea where he is or what is really happening. His last words to Sally perfectly summarize his confused memory and what cause, if any, he represents: "'Goddamm it,' the old man said in a slow monotonous certain tone as if he were saying it to the beating of his heart. 'God dam every goddam thing to hell.'"[6]

FADE TO BLACK

In movie making the term "fade to black" refers to a scene in a movie when the screen dims to a point where the projected image disappears and the screen turns black. The Lost Cause myth has not yet reached that point in the popular memory of Reconstruction. But the image has begun to fade.

Historian Gaines Foster has traced the myth through a series of defined stages. First, there was the need to understand and embrace defeat, embrace the pain, in some meaningful way. Was God on their side? Perhaps their army drank too much (which it did) or maybe there was too much "cussin" in the ranks. If not that, perhaps they were meant to undergo some great trial as a test of their virtue—a variation of the biblical story about the trials and tribulations of Job. The rebel soldiers had been brave and they had fought the good fight. In any event, the cause was good—the defense of states' rights and the Southern way of life.

The myth persisted into the twentieth century but its purposes changed and its appeal began to fade. During Reconstruction and into the early twentieth century, the myth had served to honor both the Confederate war dead and the living veterans and to present the confederate cause as both honorable and legal. (The issue of race and slavery was submerged by the emphasis on and the glorification of veterans—a memory preserved in amber.) With the rise of the civil rights movement in the 1950s, the myth took on a different tenor. Memories of the war, the rebel flag, and "Dixie" came to represent overtly a white supremacy and a fevered opposition to integrating the public facilities and public schools in the states of the former Confederacy.

Further, Foster argued that eventually the significance of the myth in Southern life eroded as the South changed dramatically, both demographically and economically, in the latter part of the twentieth century. As a result, by the 1980s, "most white Southerners displayed limited knowledge of or interest in the history of the Civil War." The memory of the war was fading and the issue of race more nuanced and complex in this new South. Confirming this observation was a public opinion survey that "found that just 39 percent of white Southerners claimed to have an ancestor in the Confederate army; another 37 percent did not know if their ancestors had fought or not. Only 30 percent of the same respondents admitted that they had a great deal of interest in Southern history." Because some 51 percent had "some interest" in the war, "by the 1990s the memory of the Civil War had not totally disappeared from Southern culture, but certainly the specificity and power of the Lost Cause dramatically declined."[7]

Nevertheless, even with the changes in the South, the myth, whole or in part, survives. In November 1996, for example, in a televised speech, South Carolina Governor David Beasley argued that the rebel flag should be taken down from the state capitol. In response the state legislature passed a bill four years later removing the rebel flag from the capitol dome and moving to a lesser position on the capitol grounds. Gone from the top of the building but not forgotten:

> As of 12:00 noon on the effective date of this act, the flag authorized to be flown at a designated location on the grounds of the Capitol Complex is the South Carolina

Infantry Battle Flag of the Confederate States of America [the Battle Flag of the Army of Northern Virginia (General Robert E. Lee's Army) the South Carolina, Georgia, Florida Department version]. This flag must be flown on a flagpole located at a point on the south side of the Confederate Soldier Monument, centered on the monument, ten feet from the base of the monument at a height of thirty feet. The flagpole on which the flag is flown and the area adjacent to the monument and flagpole must be illuminated at night and an appropriate decorative iron fence must be erected around the flagpole.[8]

And, so, the flag endures—"illuminated" at night and protected by a cast-iron "decorative fence." The South Carolina NAACP protested but to no avail.

As Hodding Carter III, a respected and progressive Southern journalist, also speaking in 1996, on his feelings on seeing the rebel flag stated: "It still grabs me ... Right or wrong, our ancestors fought, suffered, retreated, died, and were overcome while sustained by those same symbols."[9] The Lost Cause remains embedded in the Southern mind—a fading memory, perhaps, like one of those ragged battle flags housed in Southern state museums, but if the memory Lost Cause (and the associated memory of the miseries of Reconstruction) is in decline, eroded by time and change in the South, it still has a zombie-like ability to resurrect itself.

Notes

1 "The Night They Drove Old Dixie Down"

1 Historium: *The History Discussion Forum.* www.historium.com/2006. (accessed July 7, 2013).
2 James McPherson, Foreword to *The American Civil War: A Handbook of Literature and Research.* ed. Steven E. Woodworth (Westport, Conn.: Greenwood Press, 1996), ix.
3 David A. Lincove, *Reconstruction in the United States: An Annotated Bibliography* (Westport, Conn.: Greenwood Press, 2000).
4 See Vernon E. Jordan, Jr., "End of the Second Reconstruction?" Speech delivered at the Phoenix Urban League annual meeting, Phoenix, Arizona, 1972 and Christopher Paul Lehman, "Civil Rights in Twilight: The End of the Civil Rights Movement Era in 1973," *Journal of Black Studies,* 36 (January, 2006), 415–428.
5 *DeBow's Review* (January, 1861), 106.
6 Eric Foner, Foreword to Lincove, xiv.
7 Greensboro Truth and Reconciliation Commission, "What brought us to November 3, 1979?" Statement Archives. First Public Hearing July 15–16, 2005. Day 1: Paul Bermanzohn, MD. Day 2: Gorrell Pierce, May 25, 2006, http://www.greensborotrc.org/hear_statements.php. (accessed July 7, 2012).
8 Robbie Brown, "Bust of Civil War General Stirs Anger in Alabama." *The New York Times* August 24, 2012. http://www.nytimes.com/2012/08/25/us/fight-rages-in-selma-ala-over-a-civil-war-monument.html?_r=0. (accessed July 7, 2013).
9 Tony Judt, *Reappraisals: Reflections on the Forgotten Twentieth Century* (New York: Penguin Press, 2008), 198.
10 David W. Blight, *American Oracle: The Civil War in the Civil Rights Era* (Cambridge, Mass.: Belknap Press of Harvard University Press, 2011).

11 William Archibald Dunning, *Reconstruction, Political and Economic, 1865–1877* (New York: Harper & Brothers, 1907), 4.

12 The orthodox or traditional view had actually begun to form before the publication of Dunning's work. See Vernon L. "Reconstruction," in Writing Southern History, ed. Arthur S. Link and Rembert W. Patrick (Baton Rouge: Louisiana State University Press, 1965), 298.

13 Dunning, 122.

14 W. E. B. Du Bois, "Reconstruction and its Benefits," *American Historical Review,* 15, 4 (July, 1910), 781–795.

15 W. E. B. Du Bois quoted in David Levering Lewis introduction to W. E. B. Du Bois, *Black Reconstruction: An Essay Toward a History of the Part Black Folk Played in the Attempt to Reconstruct Democracy in America, 1860–1880.* (1935; New York, First Free Press Edition, 1998), ix.

16 Lewis, *Black Reconstruction,* xvii.

17 Eric Foner, *Reconstruction: America's Unfinished Revolution, 1863–1877.* (New York: Harper & Row, 1988), xxii.

18 In 2007, the American Film Institute removed *The Birth of a Nation* from its list of the 100 best movies of all time because of its pervasive and explicit racism; however, it ranked *Gone with the Wind* as number six out of 100 despite its more subdued but clearly racist attitudes. See www.afi.com/100years/movies10.aspx.

19 Margaret Mitchell, *Gone with the Wind,* 84th ed. (New York: Macmillan, 1975, 84th edn), 521, emphasis added.

20 Maxwell Bloomfield, "Dixon's The Leopard's Spots: A Study in Popular Racism," *American Quarterly,* XVI (Fall, 1964), 392. See also *Anthony Slide, American Racist: The Life and Films of Thomas Dixon* (Lexington: University of Kentucky Press, 2004).

21 Everett Carter, "Cultural History Written with Lightning: The Significance of Birth of a Nation," *American Quarterly,* XII (Fall, 1960), 355.

22 Roger Ebert, *The Great Films II* (New York: Broadway Books, 2003), 65.

23 Mitchell, 346.

24 Frank S. Nugent, review of "Gone With the Wind." *The New York Times Guide to the Best 1,000 Movies Ever Made.* Ed. Peter M. Nichols (New York: Three Rivers Press, 1999), 343.

25 Howard Fast, *Freedom Road* (New York: Duell, Sloan, & Pearce, 1944).

26 Bucklin Moon, review of "Freedom Road," by Howard Fast. *The New York Times Book Review*, August 27, 1944, 5. "Howard Fast," n.d., www.trussel.com/hf/moon.htm (accessed July 7, 2013).

27 Howard Fast, Introduction to *Freedom Road* (1944; New York: Crown Edition, 1969), quoted in "Howard Fast," www.trussel.com/hf/moon.htm, updated: 02/13/2013, (accessed July 7, 2013).

28 "Good Ol' Rebel Soldier." Lyrics quoted in http://www.civilwarpoetry. org/confederate/songs/rebel.html, April 16, 2001 (accessed July 7, 2012).

29 Quoted in Jordan Fenster, "Mine Ears hath Heard the Glory of Centuries of Civil War Songs," nhregister.com. See also Levon Helm with Stephen *This Wheel's on Fire: Levon Helm and the Story of the Band* (Chicago: Chicago Review Press/A Cappella Books, 2000), 188.

30 Robbie Robinson, "The Night They Drove Old Dixie Down," disc 3, track.1, *The Last Waltz: The Band in Their Farewell Concert Appearance.* © 1978 and 2002, Warner Brothers Records, Inc. & © 2002, Rhino Entertainment. 4 discs. See also, "The Night They Drove Old Dixie Down," Harvard University Press Blog, 24 April 2012. http://harvardpress.typepad.com/hup_publicity/2012/04/the-night-they-drove-old-dixie-down.html (accessed July 7, 2013). For lyrics, see, "The Night they Drove Old Dixie Down," 2008, http://theband.hiof.no/lyrics/night_they_drove_old_dixie_down.html (accessed July 7, 2013).

31 Warren Zevon, "Renegade," track 6, *Mr Bad Example.* © 1991, Giant Records. 1 disc. CD. For lyrics, see *Renegade*, © 1991 Zevon Music, administered by Warner-Tamerlane Publishing Corp. (BMI), "Warren Zevon: Keep Me in Your Heart," 2013, http://www. warrenzevon.org/14.html (accessed July 7, 2013).

32 Jenny Lewis, "Carpetbaggers," track 8, *Acid Tongue* 1 disc, © 2008, Warner Brothers Records. For lyrics see, "Jenny Lewis Lyrics," n.d., http://www.songlyrics.com/jenny-lewis/carpetbaggers-lyrics/, (accessed July 7, 2013).

33 Bruce Catton, *Reflections on the Civil War*, ed. John Leekley, (New York: Doubleday & Company, 1981), 5.

34 Annette Gordon-Reed, *Andrew Johnson*. (New York: Times Books, 2011), 102.

35 Hans Trefousse, *Historical Dictionary of Reconstruction* (New York: Greenwood Press, 1991), 133.

36 John Keegan. *The American Civil War: A Military History* (New York: Alfred A. Knoff, 2009), 354.

37 Edward Ayers, "The First Occupation: What the Reconstruction Period After the Civil War Can Teach Us About Iraq," *The New York Times*, May 29, 2005. www.nytimes.com/2005/05/29/magazine/29RECON.html?pagewanted=print (accessed July 7, 2013).

38 Turner Movie Classics, "Birth of a Nation, The (Original Movie Promo), Walter Huston Interviews D. W. Griffith," 2013, www.tcm. com/mediaroom/video/134463/Birth-of-a-Nation-The-Original-Movie-Promo-Walter-Huston-interviews-D-W-Griffith.html (accessed July 7, 2013). Huston played the lead in D. W. Griffith's biographical film *Abraham Lincoln* (1930). *The Birth of a Nation* is divided

into two parts: the Civil War and Reconstruction. Two families—the Northern Stonemans and the Southern Camerons—maintain friendly relations (a Stoneman son falls in love with a Cameron daughter and a Cameron son idealizes the Stoneman daughter) until the war begins and the two Stoneman sons and the three Cameron sons join the opposing sides. The younger Stoneman and two of the Camerons are killed in the war. Ben, the surviving Cameron son, a heroic warrior, is taken prisoner and sentenced to be hanged as a guerrilla. While in the hospital he meets Elsie, the Stoneman daughter he idealizes, and they fall in love. Elsie and Ben's mother meet with President Lincoln and convince him to issue a pardon. After Lincoln is assassinated and the war ends, Austin Stoneman, a Radical Republican Congressman, presses for harsh punishment of the South. Stoneman and his mulatto protégé—Silas Lynch—go south to observe Reconstruction in progress. Lynch is elected Lieutenant Governor of South Carolina and the legislature is full of blacks who have been fraudulently elected. These individuals are depicted as drunken thugs passing laws to humiliate Southern whites. Furious and despairing, Ben Cameron sees white children dressed as ghosts scaring black children. He decides to fight back by creating the Ku Klux Klan. Elsie, supporting her father, breaks her engagement to Ben. Meanwhile, Ben's sister—Flora—leaps to her death when approached by Gus, a black soldier. The Klan finds and kills Gus and leaves him at Silas Lynch's door. Lynch orders reprisals against the Klan and Ben's father is arrested. Ben and two former, but faithful, slaves rescue him and they take shelter in a cabin where two former Union soldiers live. Nevertheless, they shelter the Camerons. Elsie goes to Lynch to plead for the Camerons. Lynch demands that she marry him. Stoneman is angered when Lynch reveals he wishes to marry Elsie, who alerts two passing Klansman of her imprisonment by Lynch. Ben and Klansmen rescue Elsie and later ride to the rescue of the Camerons who are under siege from Lynch's troops. In the next election, Klansmen intimidate blacks into not voting. Whites regain control of South Carolina and the film ends with a double marriage of Phil Stoneman and Margaret Cameron and Ben Cameron and Elsie Stoneman, overseen by an image of Christ replacing bestial War with a city of Peace.

39 Quoted in Gabrielle McIntire, *Modernism, Memory, and Desire: T.S. Eliot and Virginia Wolf* (New York: Cambridge University Press, 2007), 169.

40 Paul A. Cohen, *History in Three Keys: The Boxers as Event, Experience, and Myth* (New York: Columbia University Press, 1997), passim.

2 Lincoln "Unmurdered"

1 E. H. Carr, *What Is History?* (New York: Vintage Books, 1967).
2 Harry Turtledove, *The Guns of the South* (New York: Random House, 1992).
3 Randall Collins, "Turning Points, Bottlenecks, and the Fallacies of Counterfactual History," *Sociological Forum,* 22, 3 (Sept., 2007), 247.
4 Quoted in Niall Ferguson, *Virtual History: Alternatives and Counterfactuals* (New York: Basic Books, 1997), 1.
5 Collins, 247.
6 Ward M. McAfree, "Review Essay," *Journal of the Abraham Lincoln Association* (Winter, 2005), 56–57, http://quod.lib.umich.edu/j/jala/ 2629860.0026.107/--lincoln-s-last-months?rgn=main;view=fulltext (accessed July 8, 2013).
7 Quoted in John Barr, unpublished M.A. thesis, University of Houston, Clear Lake, 1988, 69.
8 McAfree, 59.
9 Melvyn Stokes, *D. W. Griffith's The Birth of a Nation: A History of America's "Most Controversial Motion Picture"* (New York: Oxford University Press, 2007), 187.
10 Stokes, 188.
11 Bruce Chadwick, *The Reel Civil War: Mythmaking in American Film* (New York: Knopf, 2001), 153.
12 Chadwick, 155.
13 Stokes, 189.
14 Chadwick, 161, 162.
15 Stokes, 62.
16 Stokes, 188.
17 Stokes, 184.
18 Robert Lang, "*The Birth of a Nation:* History, Ideology, Narrative Form," ed. Robert Lang in *The Birth of a Nation: D. W. Griffith, Director* (New Brunswick, NJ: Rutgers University Press, 1994), 23.
19 Chadwick, 181.
20 Lloyd Lewis, *If Lincoln Had Lived: Addresses by M. Llewellyn Raney, Lloyd Lewis, Carl Sandberg, William E. Dodd* (Chicago: University of Chicago Press, 1935).
21 Quoted in James C. Bresnahan, ed., *Revisioning the Civil War: Historians on Counter-Factual Scenarios* (Jefferson, North Carolina: McFarland & Company, 2006), 306–308. Rable, 306; Symonds, 307; Prokpowicz, 308.
22 Anthony Lane, *The New Yorker* (November 19, 2012), 1. http:// www.newyorker.com/arts/critics/cinema/2012/11/19/121119crci_ cinema_lane?currentPage=2 (accessed July 8, 2012).

23 Don E. Fehrenbacker (ed.) *Abraham Lincoln: Speeches and Writings, 1859–1865* (New York: New American Library, 1989), 701.

3 "Let's Make a Start"

1 See George C. Rable, *Civil Wars: Women and the Crisis of Southern Nationalism* (Chicago: University of Illinois Press, 1989), passim.
 2 Jon D. Bohland, *A Lost Cause Found: Vestiges of the Old South Memory in the Shendoah Valley of Virginia,* Ph.D. dissertation, Virginia Polytechnic Institute and State University, 2006, 107.
 3 Bohland, 105.
 4 Bohland, 106.
 5 Bohland, 106, our italics.
 6 Bohland, 107.
 7 Bohland, 107–108.
 8 Gordon B. McKinney, "Women's Role in Civil War Western North Carolina," *North Carolina Historical Review,* LXIX, 1 (1992), 37.
 9 James Inscoe, "'Cold Mountain,' directed by Anthony Minghella," *Journal of American History,* 91, 3 (December, 2004), 1127–1129.
10 McKinney, 37.
11 Jenny Barrett, *Shooting the Civil War: Cinema, History and American Cultural Identity* (London: I.B.Taurus, 2009), 181, our italics.
12 Inscoe, 1128.
13 Barrett, 173; our italics.
14 Robert M. Myers, "It's What People Say We're Fighting For," in *Why We Fought: America's Wars in Film and Television,* eds Peter C. Rollins and John E. O'Connor (Lexington: University of Kentucky Press, 2008), 121.
15 Myers, 122.
16 Quoted in Myers, 123.
17 Myers, 126.
18 Myers, 129, our italics.
19 Myers, 129.
20 Myers, 130, our italics.
21 See Jane Turner Censer, *The Reconstruction of Southern Womanhood, 1865–1895* (Baton Rouge: Louisiana State University Press, 2003).

4 "Sunshine Headin' My Way"

1 Jason Sperb, "'Take a Frown, Turn it Upside Down': Splash Mountain, Walt Disney World, and the Cultural De-rac-[e]-ination of Disney's Song of the South (1946)," *Journal of Popular Culture,* 38: 5 (2005), 932, 936.
 2 Quoted in Sperb, 926.

3 Jennifer Rittenhouse, "Reading, Intimacy, and the Role of Uncle Remus in White Southern Memory," *Journal of Southern* History, 69, 3 (August, 2003), 585.
4 Rittenhouse, 605.
5 David W. Blight, *Race and Reunion: The Civil War in American Memory* (Cambridge, Mass.: Harvard University Press, 2001), 222–225.
6 Blight, 227.
7 Blight, 227–229.
8 Lorein Foote, *Seeking One Great Remedy: Francis George Shaw and Nineteenth Century Reforms* (Athens, Ohio: Ohio University Press, 2003), 119–120.
9 Blight, 338.
10 Blight, 343–345.
11 Leslie A. Schwalm, "African Americans and the Cost of Civil War," *Journal of Law, Medicine, & Ethics* (Spring, 2011), 21–22.
12 James Downes, *From Sick Freedom: African-American Illness and Suffering During the Civil War and Reconstruction* (New York: Oxford University Press, 2012), 23, 18.

5 Wilkes & Kennedy, Inc.

1 Heather Cox Richardson, "A Marshall Plan for the South? The Failure of Republican and Democratic Ideology during Reconstruction," *Civil War History,* 52, 4 (2005), 387.
2 Jenny Barrett, *Shooting the Civil War: Cinema, History and American Cultural Identity* (London: I.B.Taurus, 2009), 38–39.
3 Barbara Welter, "The Cult of True Womanhood," *American Quarterly,* 18, 2 (Summer, 1966), 151–152.
4 Welter, 159.
5 Elizabeth Fox-Genovese, "Scarlett O'Hara: The Southern Lady as New Woman," *American Quarterly*, 33, 4 (Autumn, 1991), 394–395, our italics.
6 Welter, 160.
7 Fox-Genovese, 393.
8 Margaret Mitchell, *Gone with the Wind* (New York: Warner Books, 1999), 639, our italics.
9 Mitchell, 393, our italics.
10 Mitchell, 811.
11 Mitchell, 769–770, our italics.
12 Mitchell, 770–771.
13 Bruce Chadwick, *The Reel Civil War: Mythmaking in American Film* (New York: Alfred A. Knopf, 2001), 189.
14 Pollard, 744.

15 D. J. de Laubenfels, "Where Sherman Passed," *Geographical Review,* 47, 3 (July, 1957), 381–395.
16 Roger L. Ransom, "Reconstructing Reconstruction: Options and Limitations in Federal Policies on Land distribution in 1866–1867," *Civil War History,* 52, 4 (2005), 364–377.
17 Carlisle Floyd, *The Passion of Jonathan Wade: A Musical Drama in Three Acts,* libretto (New York: Boosey & Hawkes, 1990), 1. The revised opera premiered in Houston, Texas in 1991.

6 "I Am Vengeful and I Shall Not Sleep"

1 Edward A. Pollard, *A New Southern History of the War of the Confederates* (New York: Gramercy Books, 1866), 753.
2 Pollard, 754.
3 George Rable, *But There Was No Peace: The Role of Violence in the Politics of Reconstruction* (Athens: University of Georgia Press, 1884), 3.
4 Michael Rogin, "The Sword Became a Flashing Vision," in D.W. Griffith's *The Birth of a Nation* in *Ronald Reagan, The Movie and Other Episodes of Political Demonology* (Berkeley: University of California Press, 1987), 219–220.
5 Rable, 1.
6 Daniel E. Sutherland, *A Savage Conflict: The Decisive Role of Guerrillas in the American Civil War* (Chapel Hill: University of North Carolina Press, 2009), 276–277.
7 Quoted in Albert Castel, *William Clarke Quantrill: His Life and Times* (1962; New Preface, Norman, Ok.: Univeristy of Oklahoma Press, 1999), 142.
8 Jenny Barrett, *Shooting the Civil War: Cinema, History and American National Identity* (London: I.B.Taurus, 2009), 47–48.
9 Barrett, 51; our italics.
10 Barrett, 54.
11 Barrett, 51–54.

7 "A Gallant Soldier and a Christian Gentleman"

1 William Blair, "The Use of Military Force to Protect the Gains of Reconstruction," *Civil War History* 52 (2005), 393.
2 For the role of the army in nation building, see Joseph G. Dawson, "The U.S. Army in the South: Reconstruction as Nation Building," *Armed Diplomacy: Two Centuries of American Campaigning* ed, Kevin Farrell (Fort Leavenworth, Kan.: Combat Studies Institute Press, 2004), 39–63.
3 New York State (Monuments) Commission, *Fiftieth Anniversary of the Battle of Gettysburg, 1913: Report of the New York State Commission* (Albany, NY: J.B. Lyon Company Printers, 1913).

4 *Blue and Gray Reunion: 75th Anniversary. Battle of Gettysburg, June 29th to July 6, 1938.* (United States Commission with the Pennsylvania State Commission, 1938).

5 Michael Judge, "A Hollywood Icon Lays Down the Law," January 29, 2011, *The Wall Street Journal*, http://online.wsj.com/article/SB10001424052748703293204576106080298279672.html (accessed July 8, 2013).

6 "Gettysburg: 75 Years Later." Our Archives (The National Archives). Remembering. www.ourarchives.wikispaces.net/Remembering. (accessed July 8, 2013).

7 William H. Price, *The Civil War Centennial Handbook* (Arlington, Va.: Prince Lithograph Co., Inc., 1961).

8 The Princess of the Moon

1 See Lyon Gardiner Tyler, *A Confederate Catechism.* (Charles City County, Va.: Hodcroft, 1929, 3rd edition). Tyler was the son of President John Tyler and the seventeenth president of the College of William and Mary.

2 "Editorial by Hon. John Temple Graves, Editor of the New York American," Document Archive, Stone Mountain Project, http://xroads.virginia.edu/~ug97/stone/graves.html, n.d. (Accessed July 8, 2013).

3 Charles Reagan Wilson, *Baptized in Blood: The Religion of the Lost Cause, 1865–1920* (Athens: University of Georgia Press, 1980), 19.

4 Cora Semmes Ives (A Lady from Warrenton, Va.), *The Princess of the Moon: A Confederate Faire Tale* (Baltimore, Md.: The Sun Book and Job Office, 1869), 1–73. Digitizing sponsor: University of North Carolina at Chapel Hill. www.archive.org/details/princessofmoonco00ives.

5 Quoted in Blight, 69.

6 Flannery O'Connor, "A Late Encounter with the Enemy," in *A Good Man Is Hard to Find* (1955; Reprint, New York: The Noonday Press, Farrar, Straus & Giroux, 1990), 134–144.

7 Gaines Foster, s.v., "The Lost Cause," in *The Encyclopedia of the Confederacy,* vol. 3 (New York: Simon & Schuster, 1993), 948–950. For an extended discussion of the subject see Gaines Foster, *Ghosts of the Confederacy: Defeat, the Lost Cause, and the Emergence of the New South, 1865–1913* (New York: Oxford University Press, 1987).

8 South Carolina Code of Laws. Section 1–10–10. Removal and Placement of Confederate Flag. www.gs.sc.gov/GS/GS-flag-laws.phtm#1–10–10, updated 6-26-13. (accessed May 13, 2013).

9 Quoted in David Goldfield, *Still Fighting the Civil War: The American South and Southern History* (Baton Rouge: Louisiana State University Press, 2002), 318.

Index

PLOT SUMMARIES

List of Film Directors

Amiel, Jon: *Sommersby* (1993)
Butler, David: *The Little Colonel* (1935); *The Littlest Rebel* (1935)
Cromwell, John: *Abe Lincoln in Illinois* (1940)
Dieterle, William: *Tennessee Johnson* (1942)
Eastwood, Clint: *The Outlaw Josey Wales* (1976)
Fleming, Victor: *Gone with the Wind* (1939)
Ford, Francis: *The Toll of War* (1913)
Ford, John: *Stagecoach* (1939); *Young Mr. Lincoln* (1939); *Fort Apache* (1948); *She Wore a Yellow Ribbon* (1949); *Rio Grande* (1950); *The Searchers* (1956)
Foster, Harve and Wilfred Jackson: *Song of the South* (1946)
Griffith, D.W.: *The Birth of a Nation* (1915)
Lee, Ang: *Ride with the Devil* (1999)
Maxwell, Ronald F.: *Gods and Generals* (2003)
McLaglan, Andrew: *The Undefeated* (1969)
Minghella, Anthony: *Cold Mountain* (2003)
Peckinpah, Sam: *Major Dundee* (1965)
Spielberg, Steven: *Lincoln* (2012)
Stevens, George: *Shane* (1953)
Vigne, Daniel: *The Return of Martin Guerre* (1982)
Willmott, Kevin: *C.S.A.: The Confederate States of America* (2004)
Zwick, Edward: *Glory* (1989)